If God forgets you, it is as though you have never existed. . . .
You are a tale told by an idiot; forgotten; annihilated.

Madeleine L'Engle

CLINGING TO FAITH
THROUGH DOUBT
AND DEPRESSION

LOSING
GOD

MATT ROGERS

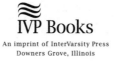

IVP Books

An imprint of InterVarsity Press
Downers Grove, Illinois

InterVarsity Press
P.O. Box 1400, Downers Grove, IL 60515-1426
World Wide Web: www.ivpress.com
E-mail: email@ivpress.com

InterVarsity Press® is the book-publishing division of InterVarsity Christian Fellowship/USA®, a student movement active on campus at hundreds of universities, colleges and schools of nursing in the United States of America, and a member movement of the International Fellowship of Evangelical Students. For information about local and regional activities, write Public Relations Dept., InterVarsity Christian Fellowship/USA, 6400 Schroeder Rd., P.O. Box 7895, Madison, WI 53707-7895, or visit the IVCF website at <www.intervarsity.org>.

Design: Matt Smith

Images: stormy sky: Terraqua Images/Corbis
   girl with hood: Ralf Schultheiss/zefa/Corbis

ISBN 978-0-8308-3620-8

Printed in the United States of America

Library of Congress Cataloging-in-Publication Data

Rogers, Matt, 1977-
   Losing God: clinging to faith through doubt and depression/Matt Rogers.
       p. cm.
   Includes bibliographical references.
   ISBN 978-0-8308-3620-8 (pbk.: alk. paper)
   1. Depression, Mental—Religious aspects—Christianity. 2.
   Depressed persons—Religious life. 3. Faith. 4. Spirituality. I.
   Title.
   BV4910.34.R63 2008
   248.8'625—dc22
                                                                2008022664

P   24   23   22   21   20   19   18   17   16   15   14   13   12   11   10   9   8   7   6   5   4   3   2   1
Y   29   28   27   26   25   24   23   22   21   20   19   18   17   16   15   14   13   12   11   10   09   08

To Kris Carraway and Jim Pace,
who stood between me and despair.
I am forever grateful.

CONTENTS

Preface

PEOPLE WRESTLING SEVERE DEPRESSION and unresolved doubts about their faith often feel isolated, as if no one in the world understands their pain. This was certainly true of me during my four-year battle. Throughout the struggle, and for years after, I searched in vain for a book I felt captured the horror of unrelenting anxiety and despair. Doubt can give rise to depression, and depression to doubt, yet the market appeared devoid of a book that acknowledged this relationship.

Most books on depression and doubt seemed written by people who had suffered neither or who failed to demonstrate how these dual struggles often intermingle. Furthermore, many of the best works on mental illness or spiritual doubt were written as information-heavy, "how-to" books, suggesting ways and means of finding freedom. While this was all well and good—education is helpful—none of these books offered much solace. What I really wanted was just to know that someone, *anyone,* had shared my pain and asked my questions—and had made it out the other side with their faith intact. I wanted a story.

I never found such a book. *Losing God* is my attempt at writing it. This is the tale of my journey through, and eventual healing from, a very long, dark night. One reviewer of this book suggested that I offer a light at the end of the tunnel sooner than I do. He wondered why I waited so long to introduce hope. One might ask the same of the biblical book of Job. Why so many chapters before a resolution?

Because that is the way the story happened.

Depression does not come with encouragement. It is a void, a vacuum, a terrible blackness. Rarely does it permit its sufferers the belief in better days ahead. One goal in writing this book was to paint a vivid and accurate picture of the *experience* of depression and doubt. Whether I have succeeded is up to the reader, but had I inserted little enticements to carry on—"Don't give up! It's going to turn out all right!"—I would have poorly served both the story and the reader because, frankly, that is not depression, and it was not my experience.

I will be quite happy if the ill walk away from this book convinced that someone else in the world can relate, and if the healthy walk away truly understanding depression and doubt despite never having endured them. For that reason, I have kept the book short but honest, introducing hope when it actually appeared. Thus, the first half of the story is dark, but it is true.

Along the way, I will comment on methods of treatment for depression and doubt, but I offer these tips within the context of my story. For readers desiring a set of steps toward healing, I offer an appendix to that effect at the end. A couple of other things to know before reading the book: (1) I talk often about the Urbana Student Missions Convention and the emotional struggle that developed there and after. I would like the reader to know that nothing negative that happened to me at Urbana was the result or fault of the conference or its organizers. Urbana has, for decades, served to ignite the hearts of young people for a life of devotion to Jesus throughout the world. I have the utmost respect for Urbana and encourage college students interested in missions to attend. (2) At times, I have changed names and minor details in the story to protect the identity of the individuals discussed. All incidents described, however, are real. Again, this is a true story.

If you have come to this book at a moment of crisis, my prayer is that you will find some comfort in what I tell here. If my story and some of the answers I found cannot end your own darkness, may they at least give you hope enough to hold on for light. The path to healing is often wet with the tears of anguished people pleading for help but not giving up when that help seems slow in coming. These people owe their peace to their perseverance. I wish the same for you.

ONE . . .

Losing God

THE BOTTOM CAME A few days before Christmas 1998. I was sitting in an old, dank theater in Charlotte, North Carolina, there to see *Life Is Beautiful,* an Italian film with a terribly ironic title. I didn't know why my good friend Baker Falls had chosen the movie, why he had driven us forty minutes from our hometown to see it, or how he had discovered this musty relic of a theater.

The movie opened harmlessly enough as a lighthearted comedy, and I wagered a little hope that the mix of happy humor and distracting subtitles would provide a couple hours' reprieve from the awful dread that now consumed me. But I was betrayed. *Life Is Beautiful,* at first a sweet, spirited tale set prior to the Holocaust, took a stark turn halfway through, as the Nazi atrocities reached the village of the film's protagonists. From there the story was a freefall to the depths of human wickedness and suffering.

Hope faded quickly as I witnessed one hellish image after another, but I could not turn away. I could not keep from staring at the screen. And I could not hide, even in the dark seclusion of this movie theater, from the demons in pursuit. For two years they had been chasing me, shouting blasphemies that were growing ever more difficult to deny. It had been two years since Urbana, since God went silent, and two years of holding back a flood of doubt and dissolution.

In a moment, near the end of the film, the dam broke. The hero of the story turned a corner in a concentration camp and found himself standing before a mound of murdered Jews, their naked, emaciated bodies piled one on top of the next. These people—*God, they were people!*—had been tossed out into some back alley like a heap of discarded mannequins from a department store gone bankrupt. The cinematographer, with frightening deftness of skill, had filled the frame to overflowing with this monument to human depravity, and all I could do was sit there

> *Either God was not good, or he did not exist, and since atheism seemed untenable, I was at last confronted with the horror of an evil God.*

as the accusations poured through my mind, flushing out the last of my resistance.

I could pretend no longer. Naiveté had led me earlier in life to believe that God was real and benevolent. Now I could see that such hope had been a child's fancy. Either God was not good, or he did not exist, and since atheism seemed untenable, I was at last confronted with the horror of an evil God. No compassionate deity would suffer his people to endure the outrage unfolding onscreen. And this was merely a re-creation, the bodies no more than a painting rendered in a special effects studio, far removed from the events portrayed.

But the events had happened. They were real. And God had not intervened. For two years I had been crying out for God to assuage my fears about his character and to settle the questions of my faith. Now this film—a damning bit of evidence—assured me that, cry as I might, there would be no answer, just as there had been none for the Jews. Anxiety began to choke me as the condemnation set in. I saw myself in eternity, wailing at the door to God's presence, knowing he would never open it to me. Like Job in the Old Testament, I was a mix of contradictory emotions, longing for God though repulsed by him.

As the credits rolled, I stumbled out into the night and fell lifeless, like one more victim of the Holocaust, into the passenger's seat of Baker's car. Minutes later, over coffee at the Starbucks next door, I unleashed on my friend two years of pent-up grief and anger, which had nowhere else to go but out. Baker knew I had been struggling since the mission convention in Urbana, Illinois, almost two years earlier to the day. Baker was a constant friend and an excellent listener, and we had talked often about my deepening melancholia. But the level of fury this night was new to both of us.

If anything I said over the next hour rattled Baker, he never let on, and I don't remember any response he might have given. Like most people, Baker was clueless as to what he should say, so he sat attentive and peaceful, just listening as I railed against the tragedy that was sapping my faith and my will to live. Baker took my suffering seriously, but he met all my allegations with the same confident smile that was his silent rebuttal. This was not smugness or arrogance on his part, nor did I receive it that way. I knew he felt tremendous compassion for me, and his smile seemed to say that despite all my confusion, somehow God was still good and life could yet turn around for me. In a mostly one-sided conversation I stated my case against the Creator, and Baker countered with just a smile.

Just a smile, but it was enough. By the time we left the coffee shop an hour later and headed for home, I was backing away from the edge. Baker's steadfast belief that there was cause for hope brought me no closer to a resolution, but it spared me a fatal unbelief that night. My tightened fist unclenched just a little, and I knew that I would hang on for another day to some distant, ethereal hope.

Collapsing exhausted into bed, I reached for my journal and the one part of my day in which I still found slight relief. Writing was therapy and the only means I had found to order the chaos in my mind, a mess of half-completed thoughts and mutinous emotions. I lay on my bed that night working with pen and paper to make sense of the day, and of the last two years. *What went wrong at Urbana, and how did it lead me here to this dead end of faith?*

* * *

I was a second-semester freshman at Campbell University, a small Baptist college in eastern North Carolina, and I was working to surrender whatever selfish desires I needed to lose to find that special calling God had for me. More than anything I wanted my life to count, to not waste it on small dreams and me-centered pursuits, so I listened to my mentors when they confronted me with the great needs of the world. Bruce and J. D. were training for overseas ministry when I met them, and they were baffled that more American Christians were not prepared to give up their comfortable lives to join Jesus on the narrow way of self-sacrifice. They could not understand believers who didn't dream of sharing the gift of salvation with the people in faraway lands where no word of the gospel and Scripture had traveled.

Bruce and J. D. talked often at our Monday night Bible studies of the 1.3 billion people on the planet who had never heard the name Jesus, and I felt ashamed that my heart was barely moved. The number was just a figure to me, an abstraction. I needed faces, individual people whose eyes I could gaze into and see the fear and darkness of humanity separated from its God. Statistics rattled off at Bible studies did nothing for me, so when the brochures for the Urbana Student Mission Convention 96 came around, offering a chance to catch God's heart for the lost, I took one and began asking God if he wanted me there the following December. I told no one back home about Urbana, deciding I should know more about it and if I wanted to go before raising the subject with my parents.

By spring, my heart was stirred. I cared little for souls beyond my tiny sphere of influence, and I was bothered enough by that fact to feel responsible to attend Urbana the next school year. The convention, however, cost $350, money I didn't have as a college student and didn't know where to find.

Over Easter break, still having told no one about Urbana, I visited my home church, happy to see the familiar faces of friends I loved and missed. Ima Jones, a kind and elegant older lady, maybe in her sixties, came over to say hello and pressed a folded piece of paper into my hand as she gave me a hug. After she had walked back to her pew, I sat down in mine and opened the paper: a check for $350!

I must have stared at that check the rest of the day. Ima didn't know why she had given it, only that she felt she was supposed to and she wanted to. But I knew why. I had no doubt, and soon I was imagining all that God would do in my life with those five days in late December.

* * *

The ride north to Urbana was torture. I was anxious the whole way, nervous about the five days in front of me and near-panicked at having found my introverted self sandwiched on a narrow bus with dozens of young, rambunctious saints, giddy on their way to a great commissioning. *I could have taken a plane.* But you'll meet people on one of the chartered buses, the brochure promised—except that most of the students on my bus came from big schools and were traveling in large groups. (Only two others joined me from our small college, a professor many years my elder and a quiet girl I barely knew who was on a different bus.) These people weren't looking to meet anyone. They were sharing an adventure with their friends, and after a few failed attempts at conversation, I shrank back into the safety of the little cell formed by my seat and the one in front of me.

All but the very last leg of the journey was in the dark, so there was nothing to see except the mountainous rock formations streaking past my window as the bus climbed into Virginia on I-77. The seats on the bus reclined a pathetic five degrees, not nearly enough to make sleep an option. Even if I'd had a bed, I doubt I could have slept: the bus growled all night as it made its way northwest, and inside, laughter broke out constantly over jokes too far up or down the aisle for me to catch. The monotony of the ride was broken only by my Sony Discman, my compact Bible and two movies—*Mr. Holland's Opus,* which I enjoyed, and *Apollo 13,* which I did not—provided by the charter company.

We stopped a couple times for food, giving me the thrill of a prisoner released from his cell for fresh air and recreation. Then it was back on board, back in the cell and back on the road to what I hoped would be some direction for my life.

Irritable from the long trip, I stepped off the bus thirteen hours later onto the muddy soil of rural Illinois. My feet sank into the saturated earth, and I wondered where all the snow was that I'd heard tales of from Urbanas-past. Only a few white patches dotted the flat, unimpressive landscape that was yellow with the dead of winter. I was cold, not from the weather, which was mild for late December, but from an uneasiness within. Anxious and unhappy, for reasons I did not yet know, I'd have rather been anywhere else but there.

After checking into my room in a dorm on campus, I walked around the university grounds with one of my roommates for the conference. I was hoping to make a friend and shake the heaviness off my heart, but the roommate was too independent for conversation. My glumness was feeling more like oppression with every step. *Why do I feel like this? I'm probably just nervous. I always get anxious in new situations. I'll feel better once the conference begins.*

In the evening we gathered, some 17,000 of us, into Assembly Hall. We worshiped and prayed to prepare our hearts as sanctuaries where God would meet with us over the next few days. My heart was unmoved. I was cold still and terribly sad, wishing to God I were back home, enjoying a normal Christmas break. *This is not how it was supposed to be . . . the $350 . . . I know I'm supposed to be here!*

I could not worship. I didn't even want to. There was a cloud over my mind and a shadow in my heart. I felt nothing but uneasiness and a sense of wrongness, like darkness closing in on a patient succumbing to anesthesia. The light in the room seemed so dim it was hardly light at all, and the sound was noise. My clapping and singing were movement without feeling. I meant none of my words. *It's been a long day. Maybe I'll feel better after I sleep. Dear God, it's been a long day!* But the morning was the same. The anxiety greeted me at dawn, a rock in the pit of my stomach. My soul was cheerless and gray, with the clouds outside my window in full agreement.

Urbana is in a rural setting, with a working farm on campus for the agriculture students, and that morning a steady breeze summoned the stench of animal waste, which mingled with the dew-drenched air. The day was so damp and putrid that the walk to Assembly Hall left my hair wet as if I'd swum through cow urine to get there. More empty songs and prayers started the day, and then it was off to small groups covering every aspect of a life on mission with God.

None of it interested me. I moved through the morning numb to everything I heard, obsessed with how bad I felt and taken by disappointment at the way Urbana was unfolding. *Why God? I'm supposed to find your heart here.*

Testimony time abounded at Urbana, and it was the most crushing, as throngs of happy saints shared rapturous tales of the glories God had shown them. I could not find any reason why the gracious revelations happened here but not back home. They were simply a benefit of the conference, it seemed, thrown in with the price of admission: you show up, grab your room key and meal pass, then meet with God. All for the low cost of $350. *I showed up too, you know. I got the key and meal pass. Did I forget to check a box on the registration form? Were visions extra?*

Young men and women stood before a "breakout" session of hundreds to renounce their sins of pornography, masturbation or homosexuality. I joined the audience in polite applause for these examples of repentance, but I could not muster enough energy for the cheers that followed each confession. I did not know why I was clapping, or why these people were better for baring their souls to the masses, or what any of this had to do with missions—or why my heart was so unmoved by it all. I decided my heart was poisonous, diseased, rotten. I just wanted to leave, to escape.

We gathered again in the evening at Assembly Hall, and the oppression again weighed heavily on my heart. The fear was overwhelming, making my blood burn like fire beneath my skin. *God, what is wrong? PLEASE tell me what is wrong!*

I sang on—in vain.

> *He loves me*
> *He loves me*
> *I can really say I know*
> *And I love Him*
> *I love—*

I stopped singing because it was a lie, because *I* was a lie. I did not love God, and I could not sing the words anymore. I physically could not sing them. Something in me died in that moment as fear consumed whatever remained of my soul. This was the fear of Judas, once a disciple of Christ, yet in an instant a traitor and a condemned man. Forgiveness dissolved into nothingness, and I felt the full weight of my sin, the guilt of a soul with no affection for its Savior. The grace I knew as a fifteen-year-old boy when I first believed in Christ now seemed a lifetime away. Had it ever been real? Had all my joy back then been a delusion? Was this the point of Urbana, of the $350, to drag me hundreds of miles from home and show me my heart's true condition before a dreadfully holy God?

I stood frozen, a child of wrath, locked outside in the cold and left to die, while a sea of saints worshiped joyfully in the chambers of the God who delighted in them. All I could do was peer longingly through the window of his house and wish I were one of the accepted. *Does God even know I'm out here? Does he care? If I knocked, would he answer?* I feared his rejection: "I never knew you."

TWO . . .
Rejected by God

MORE THAN A DECADE later, I still struggle for words that can adequately describe the terror of those five desperate days in Illinois. I never saw the sun at Urbana. Maybe it tried to show itself that first day as I stepped off the bus after a lonely thirteen-hour ride, but the gathering clouds were, by that point, already spreading gloom over the campus to match my somber mood.

Truthfully, the clouds had been gathering in my mind months before Urbana, though they were so thin and nebulous then that I had failed to notice them. It never occurred to me that my devastation in Assembly Hall was anything other than spiritual. Urbana was, after all, a mission convention, *and* the darkness had overtaken me in a moment of worship. The possibility of depression never entered my thoughts.

In retrospect, however, I can see the early warning signs from the fall semester before the convention. I remember needing an ever-increasing amount of entertainment to distract myself from feelings of discontentment. I immersed myself in activities I thought would bring pleasure, but I experienced only disappointment. The happiness a college student finds in simple things, in time spent with friends over late-night fast food, strangely and rather suddenly eroded. In its place, a profound sadness grew as I imagined a future time (still years away) when I would have to leave these friends behind.

> *If my soul is truly healthy, I reasoned, I wouldn't need friends or entertainment; I would find my satisfaction in God alone.*

None of this raised any red flags as to my mental state. If anything, my loss of joy suggested a spiritual ailment. *If my soul is truly healthy,* I reasoned, *I wouldn't need friends or entertainment; I would find my satisfaction in God alone.* Somehow I failed to consider that friends and entertainment are gifts from God, and that my desire to enjoy them was healthy. Instead, I interpreted my need for them as an ungodly weakness, a problem of the spirit that would clear up if I only loved God more.

In one of the first sermons I ever remember hearing, a preacher on television asked, "Why do you come to church? Do you come for God or to see your friends?"—the obvious implication was that God was a good motivation and friends were not. Never mind the apostle Paul's teaching on the church as a body that is to care for its members.

Never mind, even, what Jesus said were the two greatest commands in all of Scripture: to love God *and* love people. Perhaps that preacher meant we should come to church for *both* God and friends, but I filed his message away as, "All we need is God." Thus, I never questioned why I had lost my ability to enjoy leisure time with friends; I only wondered what was wrong with my spirit to have ever needed it in the first place.

Already I had a handful of symptoms doctors look for in diagnosing clinical depression. A handful more would come with Urbana: feelings of emptiness, the gloom and fear, the unattributable sense of wrongness with the world, and a total self-loathing. But I knew nothing of the growing problem in my mind. I only knew that, at Urbana, heaven had gone silent, fear had entered my heart, and the light of my life had gone out. All was darkness.

One January afternoon following Urbana, before returning to Campbell for another semester, I met my pastor, Jeff Long, for lunch. We talked about my doubts and fears and my frustrating inability to feel any love for God. I avoided specifics about the conference, not wishing to relive the horror, but I spoke in strong enough generalities that my anguish was obvious. I expected spiritual advice. Instead, Jeff only asked, "Matt, do you struggle with depression?"

I cannot recall what answer I gave Jeff, but I know that I must have quickly dismissed his suggestion because I immediately returned to searching for a spiritual cause for my darkness. I tied the nightfall not to any depressive symptoms

I had leading up to Urbana, but to Urbana itself, and to that one terrifying moment in Assembly Hall.

I love Him
I love—

* * *

Bruce, J. D. and the cast of Monday Night Bible Study were eager to hear a testimony of all God's goodness to me at Urbana. My other two companions at the conference, the quiet girl and the professor, had enjoyed their Illinois visit. I tried explaining why my story was different, why it sounded more like a tragedy, but I could see in the confused stares of fellow students that I was not getting through. I used Hebrews 12 to spin Urbana as God's disciplining me for my good, but truthfully, I was as confused as my audience. I had no idea what to make of the Urbana disaster, which was already blurred by a mind hoping to forget.

Like a victim of abuse, I was able to block the detailed memories of Urbana, but the emptiness left by my experience there never went away. My soul was heavy with disappointment that weighed on me constantly. One question kept repeating in my head: *What happened?* No matter what I was doing during those early days after Urbana, I could never completely forget the nightmare or the need to understand what it meant for my relationship with God. Doubt had entered in—*Maybe I'm not saved!*—and I couldn't shake it. I obsessed about it. Always when I prayed, the doubt was there. When I sat in church, it was there. The fear followed me everywhere, only letting up long enough for me to sleep at night. In the morning, it was back.

During my junior year at Campbell, a nearby church hosted a production of *Heaven's Gates & Hell's Flames,* and I went with friends to see it. The drama featured scenarios in which people died and stood before the judgment seat of God. People who knew Jesus were led into glory, while those without Christ were cast into fire. Lights flashed red and sinners screamed as they scraped and clawed to stay in heaven. Saved children were separated from their condemned parents. One friend went with Jesus, the other with demons. Wailing and gnashing of teeth: the imagery was horrifying.

When the lights came up at the end, the pastor pleaded with unsaved visitors to trust Christ before they wound up as real-life victims of the tragedies presented onstage. The pastor's words were sound and serious as he invited people to the front for salvation, but something more than just the tone of the evening felt wrong. I couldn't wait for the event to be over.

I had a cold at the time, and the lady in the seat next to me mistook my sniffles for conviction. She handed me a Kleenex for comfort and stopped me as I stood to leave. In a thick Southern drawl, she said with disappointment, "Oh huhney, I wuz shoowuh yew wuh gownuh ruhceive Jeesus tuhnight!"

"Ma'am," I replied, "I've been a Christian for four years."

"Oh, well PRAISE the LAWUHD!" she said with a smile, and she wished me a good night.

I hurried for the exit with my friends. I had told the lady I'd been a Christian for years, but in my soul I felt the fear. *Maybe*

I'm not. Maybe the Spirit told that lady to pray for me. Maybe this constant doubt is God's way of telling me I'm lost. Maybe that's why I don't love Jesus. On and on. Incessant introspection.

Four years' experience as a Christian had taught me I should turn to Scripture when confused about my faith, so I began racing through the Bible with feverish determination. I needed a reassuring word from God, and I knew to look for it among the pages of, what my teachers told me, was God's love letter to humans. God would speak to me there if I would sacrifice the time to study. But days passed, and then weeks that turned to months, with no change, no comfort. I groaned in my journal,

JOURNAL

THURSDAY, NOVEMBER 27, 1997

Thanksgiving day, and I sit in the center of a terrible crisis in my faith. I know I don't love Jesus. I think I have known the problem was there for a long time, but it has never been so clear as now. It's been so long since I've felt close to God, and the horror is that I have no idea what to do. I am so ashamed of me. Every day I long for a savior to change my heart, and all the while I know there is no other savior than the one my heart doesn't love.

I want to know what people mean when they say, "I love Jesus." I want to love him too. I wonder if I ever will.

Desperation kept me coming again and again to a Bible

that was dry and dead to me. I read because I did not know what else to do. I searched for answers like a castaway watching the horizon for hope of rescue. I had heard somewhere that Romans was the Christian's constitution, that if you were stranded on a desert island with only one book of the Bible, you would want Romans. I was stranded for sure, so I took up Paul's letter to the church at Rome and scoured every chapter for a lifeboat that might carry me home.

Romans 8:28 promised that "in all things God works for the good of those who love him." But that was my problem. I did not love God. My heart felt nothing for him. How could I say then that God was working anything for my good?

I could have put the Bible down in frustration then and returned sometime later to another book, maybe Psalms or Lamentations, but I drove on, unaware of the collision ahead.

> *It is not as though God's word had failed. . . .*
> *God has mercy on whom he wants to have mercy, and*
> *he hardens whom he wants to harden.*
>
> *One of you will say to me: "Then why does God still*
> *blame us? For who resists his will?" But who are you, O*
> *man, to talk back to God? "Shall what is formed say to him*
> *who formed it, 'Why did you make me like this?' " Does*
> *not the potter have the right to make out of the same lump*
> *of clay some pottery for noble purposes and some for common*
> *use?*
>
> *What if God, choosing to show his wrath and make*
> *his power known, bore with great patience the objects of*
> *his wrath—prepared for destruction? What if he did this*

to make the riches of his glory known to the objects of his
mercy, whom he prepared in advance for glory—even us,
whom he also called . . . (Romans 9:6, 18-24)

How many times before had I read that passage, yet never *read* it? How often had I listened to the words but never absorbed their meaning? "God has mercy on whom he wants to have mercy, and he hardens whom he wants to harden." This was not the Sunday-school God I had been introduced to, the loving shepherd searching for his lost sheep, faithfully loving all sinners and longing to make them saints. This God chose some and not others, and if he didn't choose you, you had no recourse, for who can argue with God? *If God has not called me, then I am not an object of his mercy, and if not an object of mercy, then I am an object of his wrath!*

My crippled soul sank into hopelessness, and the fire of Urbana burned once more beneath my skin. I was there again in that sea of saints, all happily caught up in God while I stood gnashing my teeth at the searing pain of separation and rejection. I was hardened on the edge of hell, prepared for destruction.

Everywhere I turned there was despondency and the stench of death. I could not look up for help, or to my friends, or to the very Bible that now assured me of judgment. Every day was as meaningless as the one before, and every minute was an inch closer to that forever abyss. I tried to forget, to run away, but each morning I awoke to the same fear and sadness, the loss of forgiveness.

For months I stumbled in darkness for a way out of my

misery, but there was no escaping an omnipotent God with his will firmly set against me. I knew the Bible well, that the same Scriptures that spoke of God's sovereign choice of some and not others also spoke of his wish for "all men to be saved and to come to a knowledge of the truth" (1 Timothy 2:4). But all seemed like wishful thinking, fairy-tale hope in the face of Romans 9.

THREE . . .
The Dark Side of Sovereignty

AFTER THE DEATH OF his wife, the famous theologian and author C. S. Lewis wrote in his journal, "Sooner or later I must face the question in plain language. What reason have we, except our own desperate wishes, to believe that God is, by any standard we can conceive, 'good'? Doesn't all the *prima facie* evidence suggest exactly the opposite? What have we to set against it?"

I was not yet bold enough in my suffering to declare God evil, but I was certain I could never again say with confidence that he was, in fact, good. The loss of this assurance was awful. For four years the knowledge of salvation, a sense of belonging to God, had given me purpose and joy. Richness and wonder and vitality entered my world on that November evening in 1992 when I finally understood what the cross was about, why Jesus hung and died there, and what all the talk of forgiveness for sin meant. God's love for me—for the whole world—was so extreme that God sacrificed his own son to pay for the things I had done wrong. What beautiful providence found me that night! How had I stumbled on such a treasure as God when I wasn't looking for him? It seemed that the Father had simply chosen me, and I reveled in my adoption as a son.

But then came Urbana. Now I found myself on the dark side of sovereignty, terrified and resentful of the doctrine that once brought me comfort. An election is a wonderful thing if you win, but what if you are rejected? What meaning does life hold for the *un*elect? Having had good parents, I can only guess what a person feels like who has been abandoned by a mother or father (or both). But the rejection I felt from heaven, though imaginary, did give me some idea. To believe oneself disowned by the Creator must be the deepest pain a human heart can know.

After reading Romans 9, as filtered through the disorienting fog of depression, I did not know what to make of the Bible's talk of predestination or God's adoption—or what that said about God's character. Inwardly, I detested the idea of God choosing whom he would save. For years I had rejoiced in my heavenly Father without a thought for those he might have overlooked. Countless times I had promised searching souls that God cared for them—but what if they were not elected?

At Campbell I encountered a group of students who loved to speak endlessly of God's sovereignty as if it were chief among his attributes. They boldly asserted God's discriminating love, which he lavished only on the elect, his chosen few.

Adam Dawson was a leading voice among these students. He was known around campus as something of a hermit. He came out of hiding for class and for an occasional Bible study, but he spent much of his time in his dorm room, studying Scripture, doctrine and church history. A quiet, yet eloquent intellectual, Adam talked often about the sovereign ways of God, how the only truly free Being in the universe had, before there was time, handpicked his children from among the people of the world, rejecting the rest of humanity as condemned and hopeless.

> *I hated Adam's God, a fierce and angry judge who flaunted his sovereignty and doled out salvation to whichever of his wretches he chose.*

"All the greats throughout church history taught and believed this," Adam would say.

A handful of students gravitated toward Adam, like disciples to a sage, and *predestination* became a buzzword all over campus. As students took sides, the Christian community at Campbell—at least the element of it that was aware of the controversy—splintered. With a doctrine of bliss for God's beloved and suffering for his hated foes, Adam and company won as many enemies as friends. It was no longer enough to follow Jesus; you had to choose between a God who loved the world and one who only loved the elect.

I hated Adam Dawson. I envied his confidence while I wallowed in confusion. I despised the pleasure he found in the doctrine that had devastated me. I hated Adam's God, a fierce and angry judge who flaunted his sovereignty and doled out salvation to whichever of his wretches he chose. And I feared my rage: *What if Adam is right? What if God hates me? What if the anger I throw at Adam is just projected disgust of the God who has condemned me?*

I hated Adam, yes, but I had to hear him out. If he was right, if I was at war with a wrathful Lord, I needed to know. One phone call to Adam's room, and a meeting was arranged.

Early in October of my senior year, late one evening when it was dark outside already, Adam came to my apartment, eager to talk about his passion and happy to hear my interest in learning more. He had no idea how I felt about him, and indeed, resenting the man in person was difficult. Adam was gentle and soft spoken, never brash. He smiled frequently and was always polite. And whatever his theology, Adam exuded kindness.

I talked a bit about Urbana, the hardness of my heart there, the fog and confusion, and all that had followed. Then I came to the center of it all, Romans 9 and the question of my eternal fate.

On the Scriptures, Adam was insistent: "Paul teaches that our hearts are so evil that even if we could choose to love God, we never would. God must give us grace to even desire him, and faith to believe. It is his work from start to finish. He chooses who he will save apart from any choice or will of our own, and only an unregenerate heart could suggest otherwise."

I burned with fear at the thought. I *was* suggesting otherwise. Was this the proof I had been searching for, the irrefutable evidence that I was rejected by God and unloved? "But doesn't God love everyone?" I countered, hoping for comfort I knew wasn't coming. "Doesn't 2 Peter 3:9 say that God wants everyone to come to repentance?"

Adam was ready with an answer. "Since God chooses whom he will save, the everyone Peter speaks of is God's elect. He wants all of his chosen ones to come to repentance. And Romans 9 makes clear that God does not love everyone. He loves his elect. Romans 9:13 says, 'Jacob I loved, but Esau I hated.' Jacob was chosen. Esau was rejected."

Adam was lucid and prepared, and I was no match for this budding theologian. He had me, a counterpoint for my every objection. I asked, "How can a person know, then, if God wants to save him?"

"He can only know after the fact."

By now the tide had rolled in, covering me in dark waves, and I was drowning. I did not know if I was saved. I did not love the God who *could* save me. And now I could not even know if he *wanted* to save me.

"Is it possible to be saved but not love the Savior?" I asked, terrified of what Adam would say.

"A person who has been graced with faith should find the Savior beautiful."

Jesus was anything but beautiful to me. He appeared stern and capricious, calling at random some as servants and shutting out the rest, like I had been shut out at Urbana. *How could*

I ever love a God like that? "Is it possible that I'm saved even though I feel like this?"

"The fact that you struggle," Adam said, "that you even want to love God, is evidence of the new nature. If the Spirit were not working in your heart, you would not care about God. You would not be bothered by your condition."

It was the first reassuring word Adam had said, but the hope was tenuous at best. I needed *proof* of the new nature, not evidence. And if I could only know after the fact that God wished to save me, what did my constant uncertainty suggest? In Romans 8:16, Paul said, "The Spirit himself testifies with our spirit that we are God's children." I could remember a time when that was true of me, but I hadn't heard the Spirit in two years.

Adam needed to get back to his dorm, perhaps for more studying before bed, so we ended our conversation abruptly. As he headed out my door and back to his hermit hole, Adam promised to pray for me, noting that many saints have struggled long in darkness before reaching a place in the light. It was little comfort.

* * *

The conversation with Adam lingered with me for weeks. In its wake my depression was chronic, but it was most acute whenever I was home on break. I thought this ramping up was due, perhaps, to the disruption of my schedule, the cessation of activity and busyness, and the loss of normal distractions like friends and classes and homework. But the change was so sudden! Every trip home began with excitement in the morning, followed by an uneventful three-hour drive west, during which I was remarkably stable in my thinking. Then, like crossing an invisible barrier, I tanked the instant I hit the limits of my hometown. What caused the instantaneous shift, I do not know. Perhaps it was the inevitable disappointment of realizing the clouds had followed me home, and that home provided none of the temporary escapes of college life. Whatever the cause, as I crossed the invisible barrier, the pain crystallized, came into focus, like a postoperative patient emerging from a morphine stupor. Waves of anxiety and dread crashed over me, eroding all sense of well-being, and darkness fell, covering me in hopeless despair. This happened on each of my three trips home during the fall semester of my senior year.

If I wasn't sleeping to fend off the fear, I was sitting at the desk in my old room, flipping aimlessly through Scripture, looking for any words that would speak comfort to me. One night over fall break, I opened the Bible at random, and my eyes settled on Amos 5:18 and 20, a passage subtitled "The Day of the LORD."

> *Woe to you who long*
> *for the day of the LORD! . . .*
> *Will not the day of the LORD be darkness, not light—*
> *pitch-dark, without a ray of brightness?*

I knew this was an awful way to study the Bible, that I should not simply point to a verse, ignoring all context, and assume God was speaking directly to me. But my brain was screaming at me this night, and the mental chaos lifted the words off the page and made them almost audible. I could feel God thundering at me through the passage. Every word blistered me, as even the faint hope I had for a brighter future was stolen away. Why long for a better day? That day would be darkness, not light. I spent the rest of fall break under the promise of eternal pain, with the prophecy of Amos replaying in my head again and again.

Thanksgiving that year was ghastly as well. One afternoon, while my parents were away, I caught a few minutes of a religious television drama depicting the end times and God's judgment on the unrepentant world. I thought of the people I knew who did not believe in Jesus, and my tortured mind constructed images and sounds of them writhing in hell and weeping without hope. The weight of the despair bent me to the floor, and there, in a near fetal position, I lay sobbing the whole afternoon.

Looking back, I can see now a consistency to the horror, a daily pattern that, had I been able to reason at all, should have suggested mental illness: I enjoyed an hour of clarity and calm each morning, but by midday the clouds had gathered for the afternoon storms; evenings I was partly cloudy.

JOURNAL

Saturday, November 28, 1998

It's getting harder and harder to love even the thought of God. I don't know who he is anymore. I feel like he hates me.

I'm going back to Campbell today. I just can't fake being okay anymore.

Every break ended this way, fleeing from a battlefield to the relative safety of my bunker back at school. Of course, the depression followed me, but there I could suffer it in the privacy of my apartment, not having to hide it from my unsuspecting parents. I could not tell them what was happening. Though my parents would have been understanding, my self-imposed shame would not permit me to let them in. I was swimming in guilt over my lack of joy and love for Jesus and the terrible witness I was—if indeed there was a good God who I was supposed to be reflecting anyway.

This hiding is not uncommon for victims of depression, especially men. A 2007 *Newsweek* cover story refers to the male tendency to cover up depression as a "hidden epidemic of despair." According to the article, men will use (and abuse) alcohol, drugs, work and gambling to camouflage their illness. For me, Campbell was my cover. As a resident director, I could make excuses for how I needed to cut my breaks short and get back to school early, as I did after Thanksgiving.

The waning weeks of that fall semester, though dark, were manageable thanks to routine and distraction. Preparing for exams provided mild relief, but all the while, I knew another storm was brewing. I would not be able to flee so quickly from the approaching Christmas break. I would be home for nearly a month. It might as well have been an eternity. Though there were rare moments of light that December, none of them lasted long. One morning near Christmas of 1998, I awoke to an unusual lightness of heart and a humility that permitted a little prayer. I asked Jesus to move in my life, to bring me to a place of love for him.

A short while later, however, in a Christian bookstore, I stumbled across a book by an author I knew had a special love for Romans 9 and its doctrine of election. How I wanted to put the book down and walk away, to flee for sanity's sake from the store! But my obsessive need to know the truth would not let me, so I read on as the book shot down my every objection to predestination. One evidence, the author said, that a person is saved is that he loves Christ, not his own image of Christ but the true Christ, a sovereign Christ who sends some people to hell and saves others. I failed that test on both counts. I did not love the Savior, and I certainly did not love the idea of God choosing some and not others.

Fear burned in me again as I stood in the bookstore. What little confidence I had awakened to that morning drained away, and all the questions came back. *Am I hardened against Christ? Has God himself hardened me that he might show his wrath in me? Does this mean there is no hope for me, that God truly does not love me?*

I knew that God would have been just in choosing some and not others. We are his creation, and he can do with us as he pleases. *But why would God not want to save everyone? And what am I to do with those verses that suggest he does desire to save all? Who is God?* I didn't know anymore.

Despair swallowed me, and I spent the rest of the day in deep depression. I wanted to die so I could silence my hellish thoughts, but I feared that death would be only the beginning of an eternal hell. Then the bottom came that night in an old, dank theater in Charlotte, North Carolina, watching a life play out before me that was anything but beautiful. Only my journal and Baker's smile restrained me from a fatal unbelief.

Tuesday, December 22, 1998

Will this night ever end?

FOUR . . .
Sustaining Graces

AFTER *LIFE IS BEAUTIFUL*, even Christmas day itself could not lift my mood.

Friday, December 25, 1998

How appropriate that the day Christians celebrate the birth of their Savior should be a day of terrible doubt and struggle for me. I am barely holding on.

Saturday, December 26, 1998

Laid around most of the day in fear of judgment and hell. The hardness of my heart scares me. Sometimes I feel the only way out of the ruin in my life is death.

Jesus said a time would come when people would "say to the mountains, / 'Fall on us!' / and to the hills, 'Cover us!' " (Luke 23:30). For me, that time had come. I wanted to die. But the relentless threat of God's judgment was an ironic mercy in that it saved me from suicidal thoughts. In hell, even the grace of sleep would be revoked. I would have nowhere to hide from the torment.

The second anniversary of Urbana came and went that Christmas break without any sign of the God I had lost two years earlier. The question of my salvation—*had it been real?*—and the issue of whether God was good were as real and painful as ever. I was always searching for clues that might prove I had sincerely believed in Jesus when I had first confessed him six years earlier.

With what little energy and sanity I had, I rummaged through drawers and cabinets in my room at home, skimming over old journals and papers I'd kept for who knows what reason, looking for hope that my faith was legitimate. I had been a pack rat as a kid, so it was a mess to plow through, but somewhere in a stack of mostly junk, I found several sheets of notebook paper. On these sheets, I'd scribbled Bible verses that had been especially meaningful to me around the time of my *alleged* salvation. Nearly every verse was of Jesus imploring his audience to have faith in him. I had written down John 6:47, "I tell you the truth, he who believes has everlasting life."

I believed! I must have! Why else would I have copied that verse? The thoughts and emotions from that time in 1992 were still accessible, and I knew the experience had been authentic. Jesus had become more than a story to me. But even this physical evidence, penned by my own hand and from a sincere heart, could not erase my fears. Whatever had been true years ago seemed lost, and no past experience of grace could explain away the sense of having now been rejected by God.

The depression remained, and I spent the rest of Christmas break on the living room couch, unable to find the strength for even simple tasks. Depression is, in its more severe manifestations, an all-consuming illness. It saps its victim of all but essential life energy. The thought of making my bed or brushing my teeth was exhausting; even more so were the tasks themselves. It seemed as though my body had spent all its abilities on just keeping my mind running in tormented circles. Around and around I went, day after dismal day, repeating the same dreary possibilities: *Maybe God is evil. Maybe I'm going to burn in hell forever.*

When my parents asked what was wrong, I blamed my lethargy on tiredness. "Didn't sleep well last night." That was true enough, but not even half the story. I had, during this time, a curious love affair with football. Before the depression, I hadn't cared much for the sport and almost never watched it. Now I spent hours on the couch watching game after game. Little thinking or energy were required, and each contest lasted more than three hours. This provided another excuse for why I never moved: "Have to see how the game ends." Once that excuse wore thin, I packed my things and headed back to Campbell (sooner than necessary, of course) for my final semester of college.

* * *

Rebecca Johnson had convinced me to sign up with her for physiological psychology, the study of the brain and its relationship to a person's behavior. Only premedical students and psychology majors were required to take the class. I was studying communication, which had the (unfair, I think) reputation of being the easy major, the path

It just did not seem reasonable to me that insufficient serotonin could explain Urbana or why God had shut me out.

you take once bad grades force you out of pre-law or pre-med. But Rebecca's brother, Jeff, had suffered a rare brain disorder, requiring surgery that slightly altered his personality—same Jeff, only more sarcastic and witty than before—and Rebecca and I wanted to know what exactly had happened in his brain to cause the change. That semester I learned about the limbic system, how damage to it could have created Jeff's new penchant for dry humor.

In addition, through that class, I received a meticulous education in mental illnesses, including depression, and what happens in the brains of those afflicted. I learned how neurotransmitters send messages to neurons, and these transmitters influence the way we feel. I also learned that low levels of a neurotransmitter known as serotonin can lead to the very symptoms I was experiencing: self-hatred, confusion, exhaustion, fits of sobbing, abnormal sleep habits, loss of all joy or pleasure in life. In studying for class tests, I had to memorize various groups of medications used in treating depression. One such group, the commonly prescribed selective serotonin reuptake inhibitors (SSRIs), helped the depressed brain maximize its use of what little serotonin it had.

All of this fascinated me, and I aced my exams in the class, outperforming many of the pre-med students in the room. Subconsciously, I must have had some idea, as I memorized my notes, that I was reading about myself, that I was depressed, and deeply so. But I still resisted what now seems a rather obvious fact, because I could not let go of the spiritual connection. It just did not seem reasonable to me that insufficient serotonin could explain Urbana or why God had shut me out. It was all or nothing for me, one or the other: either depression was the singular cause, or it was not the cause at all. My problem was mental or it was spiritual.

> *Depression may be more than simply physiological, and that's where other factors including the spiritual element come in, but it is never less than.*

The professor for the class, Dr. Allison, tried to challenge this false either-or thinking. I asked her one day after class, "How do you know if a problem like depression is spiritual or physiological?"

Dr. Allison looked confused, as if I'd asked a nonsensical question. "Matt, it's always physiological because people are physical beings. We have bodies. Thus, there are always physical processes happening in the brain that cause us to feel the way we do. Now, depression may be *more* than simply physiological, and that's where other factors including the spiritual element come in, but it is never *less* than."

Walking back to my apartment, I mulled over Dr. Allison's words. Acknowledging that I was depressed did not, as I had supposed, mean that my problem was exclusively chemical in nature. My struggles with God could be causing a physiological response in me that fit the description of depression.

One might expect that this realization would have led me to consider seeing a doctor about medications like those I had studied in class, but my either-or, this-or-that thinking simply shifted from determining the cause of my darkness (physical versus spiritual) to deciding on a course of treatment (medication versus Jesus). It seemed logical to me that if the root of my depression were spiritual, then the solution likewise would be spiritual. Antidepressants were, therefore, unnecessary.

My college pastor questioned whether this approach was wise. I met with him one afternoon during that final semester at Campbell. After listening to my story, full of fears and doubts about God, he only suggested, "If this continues and never gets any better, you might consider whether depression is the cause of your spiritual problems, rather than the result. I have a friend who went through something similar to what you've described. He began taking antidepressants, and he's feeling a lot better now."

I said I'd keep his advice in mind, but I didn't want to merely feel better. I wanted to know I was saved. I wanted to know God loved me, that God was truly good. How could a pill accomplish all that? And so I went on my way, terribly troubled and medication-free, in search of the God I lost at Urbana.

* * *

Sunday, January 24, 1999

The silence of this room is deafening. It eats away at me.
I'm so scared of God. He is so big. I am so lost. What should
I do? Where can I find peace? Only in Jesus, I know, but I
cannot hold onto any certainty of faith in him. What if my
faith isn't real?

I can see his love around me. Why can't I experience it
inside me?

God, I just want to cry! I just want to cry. Why can't this all
just be over? Why can't this be a nightmare that I could wake
up from?

Outside my apartment I can hear the laughter of people on a
collision course with hell, and they have no clue. Their laughter
is so hollow, so empty. There's really nothing to laugh at.

I'm so ruined because the only thing worth living for is the
one Person I cannot seem to find. And I'd go to sleep and forget
it all if I knew it would be gone when I awake. But I know
better.

Oh God, please save me! Whatever it means to be right
with you, please make me into that kind of person. I'm so lost
without Jesus.

From within the silence of my room, I begged God
often, and with great passion, to open my heart to him, soften
what was hardened, and make me like those worshipers at Urbana. Psalm 142:7 was a frequent prayer, "Set me free from my
prison, / that I may praise your name." I would ask this over
and over, but nothing changed. I still felt lost.

Lost, and pressed up against a deadline. This was my last semester at Campbell. Soon I would have to face a world that was flat and colorless after the loss of God. I had no direction and no purpose, and no means of finding any. What was I to do with a life that had no point? What was I to fill the years with when the only thing that meant anything was lost? My soul felt dead.

But there were graces during this time, small graces that could never undo my misery but that kept me from a fatal unbelief. I had worked up the courage to tell a few friends, in addition to Baker, about my struggle—one of the few wise decisions I made during this time. These friends were often the only check on my disturbed thinking, keeping it from running rampant.

Jason Lewis, one of the resident assistants I hired to work in the dorm, had suffered a short but significant stint with depression only a year earlier. He was a wonderful help to me whenever I needed a person who could sympathize. Just his presence on staff reminded me there was cause for hope. He made it through. Perhaps I could, as well.

Jason loaned me a book on the life of Oswald Chambers, the nineteenth-century preacher whose sermons were compiled after his death into the devotional *My Utmost for His Highest*. I knew that millions of Christians read the devotional every year and thought of him as an unshakable, stalwart saint. But the biography Jason gave me, *Abandoned to God,* included a chapter titled "Dark Night of the Soul," which chronicled a terrible four-year period of Chambers's life, after his conversion, when he mysteriously entered a long, black tunnel. He wrote of that time from the other side,

> *The sense of depravity, the vileness and bad-motivedness of my nature was terrific. . . . I knew no one who had what I wanted; in fact I did not know what I did want. But I knew that if what I had was all the Christianity there was, the thing was a fraud.*

I was greatly encouraged that one so revered for his walk with God had once been a fellow struggler. Chambers would have understood me, and what a pity it was, I thought, that so many of his devoted followers never saw the full humanity of their hero. I had read *My Utmost for His Highest*, which sadly includes no trace of Chambers's horror. How many could have found solace in his story?

Chambers wrote, "For four years, nothing but the overruling grace of God and the kindness of friends kept me out of an asylum"—words so true to my own experience I could have written them myself. I would have gone mad if not for the grace of friendship holding me together through those final bleak and fleeting days of college.

Natalie Hillon was often able to talk me out of despair by speaking sense into my confusion. She had the most wonderful laugh and a sense of humor that matched mine perfectly. Serious when the moment required it, Natalie could be absolutely silly when it did not. She never pretended to understand what was happening to me, but she helped me see hopeful possibilities I could not imagine on my own.

Maybe there is a loving plan concealed behind the clouds. Though neither of us could see it, Natalie imagined it and painted a picture of it for me. She looked with me into the abyss of my dark world, saw what I saw, yet came out with wisdom and smiles to share.

One Sunday, as we gathered for the morning service at church, Natalie looked at me when I came through the doors and said with gentle compassion, "I don't know why you keep coming. I think I would have given up by now if I were going through your struggle." Sundays were nearly always horrible for me, as I listened to the preacher talk in black-and-white terms about a God who was, to me, a murky shade of gray. Natalie knew Sundays were hard, and her comment was a way of encouraging me to persevere: in stark contrast to the self-condemning thoughts in my head, Natalie made me feel like a knight of the faith who was enduring fierce battles for the king.

Other friends helped in whatever ways they could. Charlie Lanier was humble and honest enough to admit that my questions were beyond the scope of his knowledge, so he had little advice of his own. But Charlie loved books, and one night while we were talking in his room, he handed me a copy of A. W. Tozer's *The Pursuit of God.* When I got back to my apartment I quickly thumbed through the book and chose a page near the middle to read so I could get a feel for the author's style. I landed on page sixty-four and started reading as I paced around my living room.

God will not hold us responsible to understand the

mysteries of election, predestination and the divine
sovereignty. The best and safest way to deal with these
truths is to raise our eyes to God and in deepest reverence
say, "O Lord, Thou knowest." Those things belong to the
deep and mysterious profound of God's omniscience.
Prying into them may make theologians, but it will never
make saints.

In disbelief, I stopped pacing and stood perfectly still in
the middle of my apartment, the room spinning around me
and my head dizzy as I tried to grasp what had just happened.
It was so random, yet so providential. *The Pursuit of God* surely
covered a broad range of topics, yet I had fallen at first glance
on the one paragraph I needed. An almost tangible sense of
Presence filled the room—a feeling, yes, but something more:
an awareness. I heard no voice, but I knew God was there and
that he had spoken to me.

Collecting myself, I fumbled for the phone to call Charlie,
who laughed delightedly at the story, happy to have played a
small role in a divine encounter. I lived off that experience
for days, often revisiting the paragraph to sustain hope. The
sensation of that moment had reminded me of a time when
peace was commonplace, and I didn't want the feeling to fade.
But something was lost with each reading of the paragraph
as it grew more familiar. The words were the same, but the
Presence was gone. Clouds of uncertainty rolled in again and
covered me in a thick blanket.

Depression is often like this, a bitter cycle of rising and
crashing. You soar for a brief period, as I did after reading

Tozer, hoping against hope that the illness has run its course and the storm has moved on. Inevitably, however, the clouds again overtake the sun, and you begin the descent. Over time, those swiftly passing moments of clarity become tinged with the grief of knowing they will not last.

I had worn myself out one Saturday afternoon on the issue of predestination and whether I was chosen, so I went for a drive to try to clear my head. When I turned on the radio in my car, an old hymn was playing, one I knew from years ago. The sun that day seemed cheerful and bright, and the lyrics blew over me like a soothing summer breeze, whisking away my melancholic moods and sending me flying.

> *Jesus ready stands to save you*
> *Full of pardoning love for all*
> *He is able*
> *He is able*
> *He is willing*
> *Doubt no more*

Exhilaration at the thought of doubting no more lifted me high above the fog of my mind. The next morning, however, I was back in the pit, depressed and cold as ever at the thought of Christ—the discriminating, electing and rejecting Christ—as my Lord. I hated the word *Lord*. As I got ready for church, I was panicked, wondering how I could survive the day with a mindset like this.

But once in my car, I turned on the radio to the same station as before, and an instrumental song was playing. As I made my way to church, I recognized the tune.

He is able
He is able
He is willing
Doubt no more

It was as though God were humming a familiar melody in my ear, "I am able, Matt, and I am willing! Doubt no more." Rising.

And crashing. The next day I learned that a friend's mom had died of cancer. The funeral was long, every moment of it a piercing reminder to my suffering brain of the decay and ruin of this world, and of the end that awaits us all. Any hope for resurrection and redemption seemed far away and hopelessly beyond my reach. I wondered the whole time who was worse off: my friend's mom, sealed in a casket for the rest of history, or me, languishing through life and awaiting my turn in the hearse.

* * *

I was already facing a death, of sorts. The last month and a half at Campbell was achingly sad, a time for grieving as I prepared for the loss of simple graces, like Jason and Charlie and Natalie. I walked from room to room in the dorms where my friends lived, offering anguished goodbyes like a terminal patient. "Have a nice life." Some of my closest friends were a year behind me in school, so they would be together again in the fall. I alone would be missing. In every way that mattered, I felt as though I were dying to them, and they to me. They would go on living and enjoying the company of one another, while I reluctantly moved on into whatever gray unknown lay ahead.

I was angry at God that none of the friends I made post-Urbana would ever see me as I was before the darkness. They would only know the shell of myself I had become, a man plundered of all the pleasure he once found in living. For months, ever since I had stumbled on the verses, Lamentations 3:25-26 had been on my heart in the hope that I might see—and that the friends who had faithfully prayed might see—a resolution to my tragedy. "The LORD is good to those whose hope is in him, / to the one who seeks him; / it is good to wait quietly / for the salvation of the LORD." I had been waiting and hoping and seeking, but it was now clear there would be no salvation coming soon.

After suffering through my complaints all evening, a friend told me one night near graduation that I sounded like a man going through a bad breakup. At the time I resented what I thought was a careless comment that trivialized my anguish. Later, however, I realized that this friend had described me exactly. Losing God had been like a divorce—it was bitter and messy—and now I was losing my friends who had been my only support through the separation.

The final drive home from Campbell was surreal. Everything was incomplete, yet at an end. The story had not resolved, it had simply stopped. The third act of the play was missing. What had been the point of all this, of sinking four years and much of my heart into friends who were now cut off from me by something so insignificant as a piece of paper, a diploma? Supposedly a degree meant I was worth hiring, but I didn't want a job. I wanted my life back. I wanted my friends to see me healed, walking in the light for which they had spent so much time in prayer.

The future terrified me. I would have a week at home with my family, then I was moving to Virginia for my first post-college job at a Christian radio network. The station's signal covered parts of three states, and I was stepping into the mid-day slot with normal 9-to-5 hours, instead of working over-nights like most DJs starting out in the business. The job was like striking gold for a communication major, but all I felt was fear and sadness. Everything was lost. God was gone, my friends were left behind, and my future was taking me to an unfamiliar place where I would have to face the darkness, alone.

FIVE . . .
Isolation

THE FIRST TIME I heard the radio station I would one day work for was on a trip to Virginia the summer before my senior year in college. My friend Jason Butler from Campbell lived in Pearisburg, and I took a weekend in July to visit him. Jason had the radio in his car tuned to the Christian station out of Blacksburg, about thirty minutes east. The signal faded in and out as Jason took us up and over the mountains of southwest Virginia, showing me the area where he had lived all his life. I tried to act impressed by the rolling hills of green around me, but it was a bad weekend. I was able to suppress the questions of my faith while I was with Jason, but sadness and loss were everywhere.

Friday evening, Jason drove us to the top of a steep hill that emptied out into a vacant church parking lot. We pulled over, hopped out and let down the tailgate of his truck so that we had a place to sit and watch the sun set over the hazy Blue Ridge. Jason had brought along his guitar so we could sing praise choruses while night fell—his idea, of course. The glassy finish of his Washburn acoustic reflected the red-orange glow of the sky on fire. I knew that a sunset should be beautiful. I could remember that much about my former life. And I could tell that it was beautiful to Jason. But I had no idea *why* it should be. Too much time had passed; too much was forgotten. All I could see was sadness painted all around me, in the sun and in the chalky blue mountains.

I don't remember the songs we sang that night, but I know they sounded mournful to me, like a dirge for a lost lover. My God, the lover of my soul, was gone. All I had left were these songs and the ache in my heart where love once was.

When the first stars appeared, we packed up the guitar and went in search of food. The Christian station bled in and out of static in the background, the signal struggling hard against the hills.

After a hike to a waterfall on Saturday and church on Sunday, I said goodbye to my friend and drove back to North Carolina. I was happy to leave. The sadness had permeated everything all weekend, and the Virginia hills were tainted now. By midafternoon, I was back at my parents' house, unaware I had just gotten a glimpse of the mountains I would soon call home.

* * *

As graduation closed in, I sent resumes to more than a dozen Christian radio outlets, most of which were small and family-owned. The station I had heard in Virginia was part of a company based in Blacksburg with a vast coverage area from the many towers spread around. *Probably too big for a first job out of college, but why not send them a resume and see?*

I sent my information on a Monday, they received it Wednesday, and the general manager called that afternoon. His message on my voicemail said he wanted to talk to me, that there "might be some opportunity here for both of us." Their midday on-air announcer had just left to take a job at another station within the company, and the timing of my resume's arrival "seemed providential."

I never thought they would call.

No other station did.

I cried most of the way to Virginia. The night before, I had packed what necessities I could fit into my little Dodge Duster, and now I was making the three-hour drive north, alone. My parents would join me the next day with the rest of my things, but for now, I was utterly alone. Campbell, and the friends I had made there, now seemed a lifetime ago, like I had stepped into someone else's world where everything was new and terrifying to me. Why had I taken this job? The pay was lousy, but I had few options: remain at Campbell where I had no job, stay at home faking smiles all day while I tried to find work, or take a chance on the one radio station that had offered to hire me. I decided to take a chance.

Jon, the program director at the station, had asked in my interview if I had ever been through a significant trial and how I had handled it. I told him everything about the depression, my struggle to understand predestination, and the uncertainty of my salvation, hoping he would think I was crazy so I could avoid the scary step of moving to Blacksburg. But he was undeterred. Jon was diabetic and had once spent an entire year in the hospital; he understood depression. He ended the interview by telling me I should continue to pray, and that they would do the same and would call me if they were interested in hiring me. Given the small salary they were offering, I suppose they didn't have much of an applicant pool from which to choose, so an offer came only days later. I accepted; then declined; then called back to accept again. (How did they *not* think I was crazy?)

After paying the start-up fees on utilities, the security deposit and first month's rent on my apartment, I had three hundred dollars left to my name to tide me over till the first meager paycheck. I arrived in Blacksburg sometime in the afternoon on a warm and rainy Friday in late June, wrote the necessary checks to get my key, then unloaded my belongings at the new apartment. I was terrified—not so much by the financial hole I had just dug for myself or by the new job I would begin on Monday—but by my desperate mental condition.

Unrelenting sadness that seemed to have no bottom kept me constantly on the verge of breaking down into a crying fit: My friends were now dead to me; I was alone in a new town where nothing was familiar, nothing was home; God was far away; and I had done this to myself. I had gotten up that morning, showered, piddled at a breakfast I was too nervous to eat, and then had driven myself off a cliff of my own making.

One simple grace held me together that first day, and for a

week it had been the only bright spot on the calendar, the only thing I had to look forward to. Jason Butler was going to drive in from Pearisburg to be with me on my first night in this new place. He arrived late in the evening, and how good it was to see a friend's face! I needed conversation, so we talked over dinner at a restaurant in town.

True to his nature, Jason was quiet and unemotional as I spilled my usual woe. He was accustomed to hearing my problems, and he must have prepared himself for them on the drive into town. As we sat in the hard, wooden booth in the restaurant, Jason tried to encourage me, saying, "Matt, God is up to something in your life. I don't know what, but he's getting ready to do something with you, and it's going to be great."

Few people at that time could have said something as simplistic without invoking my absolute frustration. After three years of undiminished gloom, I needed more than breezy optimism. But I knew Jason well and respected his life, and he always spoke with a humble confidence that was neither arrogant nor trite. He was so cautious with whatever he said that I was able to receive it. I could not fully internalize his words, but I tried; I wanted to believe them, though I didn't see any hope in my future. Then again, Jason was able to sit with me on that first night, so I wasn't completely alone. Maybe that meant something.

After dinner Jason returned to Pearisburg, as he had to, and I headed home—it would be a long time before I would call it that—to my dark apartment. I don't think I slept much that first night, and I was a wreck the next day, absolutely nasty to my parents when they arrived in Blacksburg with the rest of my possessions. Having seen my despondency the week before the move (which they interpreted simply as nerves), they decided, just between the two of them, to load their living room furniture into the U-Haul and surprise me with a couch and two chairs. It was charity for sure and was the only thing saving me from sitting on the floor of an empty room when they left. Except for a bed, chest of drawers and a small desk, I had no furniture of my own.

I tried hard to work up the gratitude my parents deserved. I wanted them to see a thankful son, but I could not bring the feeling to the surface. My head was stirring and seething. I wore a scowl all day and snapped often. Every time I said a mean word, I chided myself inwardly, hoping I could snuff out the volcano brewing in me. But the eruptions were involuntary. I wanted to be nice but couldn't I was so miserable. The slightest thing set me off, and before I could bite my lip, some sarcastic comment or biting criticism escaped. I was completely guilt-ridden about it, like I had wasted my parents' day (and their furniture) on an ingrate of a son. Only I *was* grateful. Or at least I wanted to be. I struggled all day to force good feelings, but they never came. This was among the most frustrating elements of my illness: the full knowledge that I was behaving in awful ways but with a total inability to stop.

My parents left by evening, having hiked my belongings up three flights of stairs. After they drove away, I sank defeated into my surprise couch and stared blankly at the walls as the living room grew dark from daylight fading outside my window.

*   *   *

Blacksburg sits in a valley, and my melancholia made the mountains all around seem sinister. I felt caged, and I wanted to break out, but I had nowhere to go. My apartment was a dismal, little hole. The walls were white and textured, so I scraped myself if I rubbed up against them. The carpet, which was described over the phone as "sculptured Egyptian gold," looked more like steamrolled mucus green. Stains dotted the floor, and a couple decades of traffic had leveled its "sculptured" pattern. The air conditioner sounded like a small aircraft so that whenever it roared into action I had to up the volume on the radio or television. The place had scant lighting, and it gave the walls a yellow tinge in the evening. I had no pictures to hang and no money to buy any, so the walls were bare. It was a sad lot to call home.

The radio station where I worked was similarly decorated: bare, white walls; dingy carpet (though at least brown by design); and fluttering, florescent lighting that washed out what little color was spread around the building. I spent most of my time in the on-air studio, and it was a disaster. All the wiring—endless feet of tangled and meandering blue and white and orange and red wiring—was exposed and hanging beneath the soundboard, covered in years of dust. The shelving was cluttered with old music logs, books and broken trinkets—like the cracked Christian Coalition mug, also collecting dust, that had never made it to the trash can. The air-check machine, which recorded our shows, was so jerry-rigged that no one was completely sure how it worked (when it did), and the same could be said of the other equipment in the room. How we were broadcasting anything farther than the parking lot was a mystery, but somehow, every day, thousands of faithful listeners in three states heard my voice emanating from this engineering accident.

The studio wasn't the only thing broken at the station. After only a few days on the job, tensions among the employees surfaced. A feud had broken out months earlier between management and staff over who got what job and why. The two sides were in a stalemate by the time I arrived, going about their jobs but suspicious and distrusting of each other. Representatives of both positions tried to recruit me for their cause. Jon, the program director, who had hired me and been so understanding of my depression, wisely counseled me to do my job and ignore the drama as best I could. He was involved in it only by default. Management had brought Jon in from Canada and had given him the job of program director over another guy on deck at the station. They hired from without rather than promoting from within, and it touched off a war. We were infected with the same scraping and grasping after

Is anything accidental in a predestined world? . . . Should I assume the happy moments are providence and the bad moments are accidents?

power and position as any other office.

The station was listener-supported, and twice a year we held fund drives called share-a-thons. Listeners called in with tearful testimonies of how a special song or Bible verse had lifted their spirits at a critical moment, and we eagerly aired these phone calls as evidence for why everyone should make a donation. *Call right now! Volunteers are ready to take your pledge!* But as soon as the microphones were off, the usual vitriol filled the room. I always felt I needed a shower after share-a-thon.

* * *

Every minute of that first month was grave. I teetered on the edge of a meltdown, anxious and depressed. I was a frightened child, wandering confused through a grown-up world. And the problems from Campbell had followed me to Virginia.

JOURNAL

Monday, July 26, 1999

It is a terrible emptiness in my soul, this unexplainable absence of conscious fellowship with God.

Almost as terrible, and equally unexplainable, was the silence of loved ones. Because I was alone in Blacksburg without any fellowship to fill my free time, I poured out my heart in e-mails to friends and waited anxiously for replies that sometimes never came. To a college mentor I wrote:

I feel like I've lost the only thing worth living for: my God. Can I ever again feel that passion I once felt? What is my motivation to keep walking except the fear of not? First John 4:18 says that "perfect love drives out fear, because fear has to do with punishment." I used to have no fear of God because I knew his love. Now there is much fear, which torments me.

I don't talk about this with many people. But I knew you would pray, that you might have some wisdom to share, and that you would not be made to stumble spiritually by this discussion. If in any way I have caused you to stumble by writing this, I am sorry. But I live with this every day and need help.

Silence. There was no answer.

Evenings were especially difficult. After work I ate my dinner in solitude, often with a side of tears, then caught an hour or so of whatever television channel I could pick up with rabbit ears. (I had no money for cable.) I e-mailed friends and read books to pass the time before bed. I tried reading the Bible but found it felt like walking through a field of land mines. If I stepped on a verse about predestination and God's electing, I would blow up and then spiral down into a terrifying state that might last for days. And with the deepened depression would come the doubts, the questions, relentless in their interrogation. *Was my salvation real? Did I really meet Jesus?*

I learned quickly that the radio in my room could also be a land mine. One night I flipped it on just in time to hear a preacher say, "God chose those he would save." I froze in fear for a second, then flipped the switch off and waited for the inevitable condemnation: *What if you just silenced the voice of God? What if he was speaking and you just hardened your heart against his Word?*

The fog and confusion had muddied my understanding of God's sovereignty and frustrated my attempts at accurately interpreting events around me. I could not distinguish the signs that meant that God was speaking from those that were mere happenstance. *Is anything accidental in a predestined world?* I could give thanks for the times I turned on the radio at the right second to hear the song I needed in that moment. But what about times like this when I turned on the radio at exactly the *wrong* second to hear the very *last* thing I needed? *Should I assume the happy moments are providence and the bad moments are accidents? A little too convenient. Better to leave the radio off and avoid sovereign moments altogether.*

In these times, it was the compassion of the saints through literature that filled the void and sustained me many nights. I copied in my journal the quotations I found helpful.

JOURNAL

MONDAY, JULY 26, 1999

"There are times when things look very dark to me—so dark that I have to wait even for hope. It is bad enough to wait in hope, to see no glimmer of a prospect and yet refuse to despair . . . to have a vacant place in my heart and yet to allow that place to be filled by no inferior presence—that is the grandest patience in the universe."—George Matheson

Time alone with my books was productive, and solitude was not quite the torture I had expected before moving to Blacksburg. It was hard and lonely, but also somewhat therapeutic in helping me process my questions. At Campbell, I was constantly yanked between two opinions. Friends on both sides of the predestination debate—does God choose us, or do we choose him?—ensured my constant confusion. They were trying to help, I know, but my pastor, Jeff, back home rightly spoke of them when he said, "Some people know just enough about that subject to be truly dangerous."

Blacksburg brought isolation to my life, but also refuge—perhaps, early on, its only grace—room to breathe and to face my questions without the propaganda of either camp ringing in my ears. Still I was alone, and this was a bitter pill on nights when hopelessness took over.

Most of the music in my life at the time was from the radio station and came in the shape of simple, happy worship tunes. All day long I had to play cheerful songs of Christian bliss that were salt in my open wounds, and I wondered if I might be the only struggler in the church. Once in a while I found evidence that I had company.

Among the few perks of my job were the CDs that record companies sent as gifts to persuade us to play their artists. A heart-wrenching hymn by Rich Mullins, called "Hard to Get," was my broken prayer in those times. One evening after work I sat in my car and feasted on the refreshing honesty of Nichole Nordeman's CD, *Wide Eyed*.

Even fields of flowers
Dressing in their best because of You
Knowing they are blessed to be in bloom
But what about November
When the air is cold and wet winds blow
Do they understand why they can't grow?

This was the dark side of sovereignty. Jesus had promised to clothe his people in the same way he clothed the flowers. *But what about the winter months when everything is dead, like I am dead? Does he love us for a season only?*

Near the radio sta-

> *All day long I had to play cheerful songs of Christian bliss that were salt in my open wounds, and I wondered if I might be the only struggler in the church.*

tion sat a cemetery, and whenever I drove by I would look at the headstones and think of all the souls whose season had ended. I would watch people in the other cars and wonder how they could pass within feet of such decay and still chatter away on cell phones like their lives even mattered. *Do they think they can talk their way out of joining the dead masses lying in the ground next to them?* I wanted to yell at them, *Don't you know you are headed there too? You will die. You will be shoved in a hole and smothered with dirt, and you'll rot there as another generation has its turn at pointless conversation.*

I thought constantly of death and endings, of November's coming. I was stung deeply, and repeatedly, by the inescapable fact that I was dying, and my friends were dying, and my family was dying; everything and everyone was dying. From the moment of conception, every child has a date with the grave. Every marriage begins with the vow, "Till death do us part." Nothing is permanent, nothing lasts. Everything with a beginning has an ending.

I drove past the cemetery and pictured myself sealed in a casket, buried underground, while the world above carried on without me. And I thought, *It isn't that long from now.* I imagined the day I would bury my parents, and I felt such an awful sadness at the thought, aloneness and emptiness. *I cannot bury them! I cannot cover them with dirt!*

This morbidly obsessive thinking is familiar to many sufferers of depression. Darkened hearts wonder why no one can see the world "as it really is." Such a dreary mindset can breed, first, revulsion at death as all there is, but then a longing for it, for relief—a longing that sometimes turns to planning. In the absence of a reprieve from excruciating mental pain, death, which one can hardly stop thinking about anyway, can seem like a reasonable way out. Every year, more than 30,000 people in the United States decide it is, and they take their own lives.

One Monday, soon after moving to Blacksburg, I came in to work at the radio station and learned that a local pastor, whose sermons we aired every Sunday, had committed suicide over the weekend. I knew the man. I had helped him record the introduction that played each week before his message. Apparently, he had endured years of serious, chronic depression, and he had left a note before his self-destruction. In the letter he apologized to his family and congregation but said he could not handle the pain any longer.

What had finally convinced this man that life wasn't worth the struggle? He was a pastor, a shepherd who had obeyed the Lord's call. "Whoever believes in me," Jesus said in John 7:38, "streams of living water will flow from within him." How many times had this tormented minister quoted his Teacher, waiting for the waters to come? How many years had he suffered before concluding they never would? This servant of God invested years—decades, perhaps—pursuing and preaching the faith, only to conclude in the end that the masses were deluded in their happiness. Was I on a similar course? How long before I concluded the same? I had been spared, up till now, any serious thoughts of killing myself, mostly because I feared I was going to hell, having lost the Savior. Could I count on the anxiety holding? How long can such a slender "mercy" save?

SIX

Search for a Cause

I WOKE UP SCARED, not only for myself but also for Brett Mitchell, a friend from years back who had called the night before to confess his own battle with fear and darkness. I had known for a year or more that Brett wrestled with his moods, and we had discussed at times my slide into confusion. Brett, however, had always seemed on top of his struggle, happy and well adjusted with only minor troubles. Now he was a freshman at a college near Blacksburg, and the move away from home had sent Brett spinning toward the edge. His every word matched my experience. The questions and doubt, the sadness and sense of wrongness about the world, the fear that burned like fire beneath the skin—it was all the same.

Brett was panicked, "This is not something to laugh about! This is serious!" He had always been a joker growing up, and we had shared a lot of laughs. Now the humor was dead.

I lay on my bed, staring at the ceiling and talking to Brett for an hour, maybe longer. I must have been thankful that someone else in the world understood my horror, but mostly I was grieved. How had two friends, both happy in their youth, been so crushed by adulthood? Had life always been terrible and we just didn't see it? Were we blinded by our childishness?

Brett's phone call gave me the sensation of falling, of plummeting back toward the abyss, losing the little altitude I had gained by my seclusion in Blacksburg. I felt confirmed in my long-held suspicion that the world was very dark; the happy masses were, as I'd feared, deluded in their hope for tomorrow.

"If I weren't so weak, I could handle life better. If I were a stronger Christian, I wouldn't need drugs."

Before hanging up, Brett asked if he could come to Blacksburg for the weekend so he didn't have to be alone with his thoughts. Of course, I said yes. Then we prayed for each other over the phone. We had never done so before, but this night was different. We needed solace we could not find in ourselves.

Brett prayed, "God, we're scared!" It was all either of us needed to say.

The next day I wrote to Natalie,

*Found out last night that a good friend is dealing with the
same thing, and I've been so down today because of it.
I would get counseling, but I don't think there's a person
on this planet who can explain what's wrong with me.
Only God knows what Urbana was about. Only he knows
why this darkness. But the Wonderful Counselor isn't talking.
I keep saying to myself, "There may be a beautiful reason for
all of this, and you wouldn't want God to cut short the work
he is doing." But some days it's just tough to keep holding on to
that. "If only I knew where to find him . . . " (Job 23:3).*

My journals and e-mails from this time are laced with quotations from the book of Job, the story of a blameless man who suffered unimaginable loss. I had been reading Philip Yancey's reflections on Job in *Disappointment with God.* "Despite what had happened," Yancey writes, "Job could not bring himself to believe in a God of cruelty and injustice. . . . Job saw the darkest side of life, heard the deepest silence of God, and still believed."

Satan was the one who'd brought the accusation before God that Job only served God because it was convenient, because God had blessed Job greatly. Take it all away, Satan charged, and Job would curse God to his face. So, in order to prove a point about God's worth, God allowed Satan to take away Job's family and possessions, and later his health.

Why? Why did Job have to pay for Satan's accusation? Why did God feel the need to justify himself and prove his worth to a fallen angel? And what of the worth of Job's children? Were they merely collateral losses in a wager between God and the devil?

The questions were strangely comforting. Before my descent into darkness I had approached the Bible as a book of answers, and it had always obliged. But Urbana brought questions the Bible didn't seem to answer in the clear and systematic ways I wanted. At first I assumed that I was to blame. *I must be reading it wrong. The Bible answers Adam Dawson's questions. Everything is clear for him.*

Then there was Job, a man like me who was following God as best he knew how when, for no apparent reason, the lights went out. Job mourned in his devastation, having lost everything that meant anything to him. Death would have been a mercy. Instead, life was the one thing left to Job.

"Why did I not perish at birth, / and die as I came from the womb?" Job asked (3:11).

His friends only stoked the fire, telling Job his sin had brought God's wrath.

"Miserable comforters are you all!" Job cried (16:2).

I had my share of Job's friends, ready to "comfort" me, able to find a sin behind every struggle. An acquaintance had e-mailed me to say, "Spend time in the Word every day, and trust God. Depression is natural, but it really isn't believing what God can do."

A week before that, another person had written, "I don't

know what to say. Give God glory. He's worthy of it!"

Yet another e-mailed, "Lack of peace and assurance only disturb us when fellowship has been broken. Sin is sin is sin, brother!"

Have these people never read the book of Job? "Miserable comforters!"

Out of all the destruction, the one unbearable pain that turns up repeatedly in Job's laments is the terrible, unexplainable loss of God, an emptiness of soul that I knew well.

"If only I knew where to find him; / if only I could go to his dwelling!" (23:3).

Job understood the darkness and fear, the fog and confusion. He searched for clear and systematic answers, and he experienced silence out of heaven. "When I think my bed will comfort me / and my couch will ease my complaint, / even then you frighten me with dreams / and terrify me with visions, / so that I prefer strangling and death, / rather than this body of mine" (Job 7:13-15).

I knew these dreams of Job. Sleep had been an escape, darkness within the darkness, where I could hide from the horror. But lately all my thoughts, whether waking or sleeping, had been dim and restless. I awoke one morning to the realization that my dreams the night before had all been disturbed. They weren't nightmares exactly but remembrances of bad experiences from the past, a stream of dreary memories strung together into dreaming.

As I showered and dressed for work, I noticed it again. I was daydreaming, not about good times past or hopes for the future, but about the bad times, wrongs I had committed and could never make right, and sad events that had happened by no fault of my own. My childhood had been relatively normal, with no major sin or trauma that should have sparked this theater in my mind, yet one after another, the cheerless episodes of my life, however slight or insignificant, replayed with vivid, painful detail. There were no happy scenes; they had all been cut.

I looked for a connection between these episodes and my spiritual sufferings, but none of the dreaming or daydreaming carried any religious overtones. I watched myself as a little boy catch his first fish and carry it home to show Mom, not realizing this meant death for my scaly captive. Excitement turned to grief as the fish gulped the air in vain, gasping out his last until his convulsing stilled and his dead, accusing eyes bore a hole through my guilty conscience. What kid hasn't caught and killed a fish, and what was the big deal anyway? Yet as the scene replayed, I was that little boy again, and I felt the same intensity of remorse as I had all those years ago, as if I'd only gone fishing the day before. I could not stop dwelling on the crime and a thousand other similarly sad moments.

What is wrong with me? If this sickness were spiritual, if the fog and confusion had followed me into my dreams, I would have expected to see Assembly Hall, or Adam Dawson and his disciples, or a mound of dead Jews on a movie screen in Charlotte. Instead, I was castigating myself for the murder of a fish when I was five.

Was my sickness more of the mind than of the soul? Was

Brett Mitchell's? He had no Urbana to blame for his misery, yet he was wholly, unutterably miserable.

Friday, August 27, 1999

My day began with a phone call from Brett at 7:30. I was just waking up. I noticed immediately that Brett sounded shaken and nervous. At first I thought it was just the way he sounds early in the morning. But then Brett told me he was going home this weekend and would not be able to come to Blacksburg as he had suggested when he called on Monday. It seems that Brett had been taking an antidepressant called Paxil, and, this past summer, Brett told his doctor that the Paxil wasn't having much effect. The doctor wanted him to take a higher dosage, but Brett decided instead, unwisely, to wean himself off of Paxil before heading to college.

Monday night's phone call made much more sense now. He was suffering significantly from the sudden changes in his brain. This morning, Brett said that he was confused and couldn't think straight. Indeed, he sounded disoriented. He said Paxil gives him a choice to not feel condemned, and, "Right now, I definitely don't have a choice."

* * *

Paxil belongs to the group of antidepressants known as SSRIs, which I had studied in physiological psychology during my final semester at Campbell. Besides Brett Mitchell, I had met one other person who took Paxil.

Kris Carraway worked in the human resources department of Trans World Radio, a missions organization that broadcasts sermons into countries closed to other forms of evangelism. Trans World was based out of Cary, North Carolina, not even an hour from Campbell, and I called one afternoon during my senior year of college to see if they might have a job for me after I graduated. The woman responsible for hiring was on leave at the time, so the next person, Kris, invited me to Trans World's headquarters for a tour.

By the time we finished the textbook trip around the building, it was clear I would not be able to work for the ministry. Their only radio broadcasts were of recorded sermons, translated into native languages; they didn't need English-speaking on-air announcers.

Talk then quickly turned to where my life was headed, which of course, led to discussion about Urbana and the confusion that had followed. I intentionally kept the conversation vague, but Kris seemed to understand anyway. With little knowledge of my past or present, she spoke with wise precision, as if I had told her all the details. "Matt, it sounds like you might be entering into a dark time in your life. You need to find a friend to whom you can say anything, and who won't be shocked."

Kris told me her story of serving overseas in missions with her husband, and then of the tumultuous seven-year depression that followed her return to the States. She spoke fondly of the friends who had listened without judging and of the medication that had restored her sanity over time. Unashamed and not self-conscious, Kris said she still took 20 milligrams of Paxil each day to maintain mental equilibrium.

At the time, what had most encouraged me about my encounter with Kris was the seemingly providential way we had met—what if the woman usually responsible for hiring had not been on vacation?—and the way Kris had seen straight into my soul, as if God had given her special insight about my life. But now, in light of my conversations with Brett Mitchell and his experiences with Paxil, combined with having studied the drug in school, I began to wonder whether God had been speaking something else that day at Trans World Radio. Had he been laying clues for me concerning medication for depression? Kris had regained control of her mind after taking Paxil; Brett had nearly lost his after going off of it.

> *Kris says she is certain of my salvation, that only people who have known the joy of total forgiveness can understand the horror of feeling that it's been stripped away.*

Has God been speaking to me all this time?

I decided to risk sharing my story—the whole story—with Kris. I wrote a four-page letter detailing the major events of my descent into darkness: Urbana, Romans 9, Adam and his disciples.

"Am I not one of the elect?" I wrote. "Does God choose not to save some people? How do I love a God like that?"

On I went for four pages, ending the letter with the most subtle of cries for help: "I would be curious to know what you think."

I was far more than merely curious; I was desperate for a reply. I came home on my lunch break every day and checked my answering machine to see if Kris had called. Finally, one day, there was a message: "Matt, I wish I had known sooner what was going on. We'll talk more later, but I want you to know I love you and you are loved by a lot of people here, and you are never going to have to walk this way again."

* * *

WEDNESDAY, SEPTEMBER 8, 1999

Kris and I have talked. She read the letter that I mailed her, and though it was filled with questions about Urbana, my salvation and predestination–deeply spiritual matters–Kris was quick to say that she does not think my problem is spiritual. My words, she said, sounded like something she could have written during her depression. Kris feels that my trip through the night is mostly mental, and only affecting me spiritually by robbing me of the ability to think right thoughts and experience the emotions of freedom in Christ. And while I may have serious doubts, Kris says she is certain of my salvation, that only people who have known the joy of total forgiveness can understand the horror of feeling that it's been stripped away. That, she points out, is evidence of a true heart change. Kris admits she is not a counselor, but she does feel that I should consider seeing a Christian psychologist, and that medication might be helpful.

Nothing definite came from our conversation, just a lot of encouragement from someone who has been through the night.

I wanted to trust Kris, to believe my hope lay partly in a prescription. But even having studied SSRIs and other medications for depression, I still had questions. *What if I take an antidepressant and it lulls me into thinking I am saved because I feel better? No one had Paxil in Jesus' day, yet he told people not to have an "anxious mind" (Luke 12:29 NKJV). By considering medication for anxiety and depression, am I shifting the blame for my problems to a mess of chemicals in my brain? Pointing the finger at my serotonin levels seems like a cop-out. If pain is the body's response when something has gone wrong, how will masking the pain solve whatever is causing it? How can Kris be sure my condition isn't primarily spiritual when my soul is so affected?*

My questions, while sincere, were largely the result of ignorance regarding both faith and psychiatry. Though I had studied antidepressants in college, I had observed few people—really only two—who had ever taken them. I had little real life experience, none of it personal, by which to judge how my mind and faith might benefit from medication. Most doctors will say that medication alone is rarely an answer, that counseling is usually needed as well. But counseling will have little effect until the mind is brought to a point where reasoning is possible. This is the goal of antidepressants.

Yet I know many, many people—intelligent, educated, rational people—who think and speak of these drugs as if they are voodoo medicine, the product of witch doctors. I've known a host of otherwise compassionate Christians who have made absolutely devastating comments to loved ones battling mood disorders.

A college-educated worship leader at a church I once visited told the congregation about a conversation he had had with his sullen grandmother. "You don't need pills, Grandma," he said, "You need Jesus!"

Since I never met her, I don't know what the lady needed, but I bet her answer was not as simple as Jesus versus medicine. The worship leader meant well, of course. He thought he was helping. It seems he simply had not considered how his healthy brain might be permitting him feelings of peace and happiness in Jesus that were being denied to his potentially serotonin-starved grandmother.

I cannot count the conversations I've had in ten years in which a person has made a disapproving face at the mere mention of medical treatment for depression. Often this response is tied to a strong belief, however unfounded, that mental illness is not an illness at all, but rather moral weakness, a refusal to accept and deal with the real world like everyone else. Psychiatry, accordingly, is seen as a pseudomedicine in which patients dope, numb and sedate themselves in a drug-induced, medically sanctioned avoidance of life's problems (ironic, given that antidepressants can actually help patients have the mental fortitude to *confront* their problems). The result of this kind of thinking on those receiving treatment is crushing: "If I weren't so weak, I could handle life better. If I were a stronger Christian, I wouldn't need drugs."

Victims of mental illness often are, as I was, fragile and

confused, with limited ability to distinguish truth from error. They are easily damaged by well-meaning people who assume they understand the world of the mind and emotions better than they do. Had that worship leader taken time to learn about depression, its treatments and its effects on the experience of faith, he might not have added to the grief of his already-hurting grandmother by weighing her down with unnecessary, unwarranted feelings of guilt and failure. He might have paused before lecturing her tormented soul.

Thankfully, Kris never lectured me. She understood my ignorance and patiently prodded me toward reason.

JOURNAL

SUNDAY, SEPTEMBER 19, 1999

I've been able to run by Kris some of my questions about medication. She doubts Paxil (or any of the SSRIs) could dupe someone into a false sense of having been saved. The drug simply gives Kris the ability to think more clearly and have rational thought processes. It doesn't make her feel a certain way or believe anything in particular. She says people who cannot think clearly are going to have a hard time sensing peace or obeying the command to not be anxious because they're telling an unhealthy brain to do things only a healthy brain can. And Paxil is not a sedative, so Kris says it cannot cover up or in any way ignore the "real problem." On the contrary, it can help a person think sanely enough to begin dealing with problems.

But how can Kris be sure my problem is bad brain chemistry and not spiritual trouble?

"Matt," Kris said in one of our frequent phone conversations, "I know you think that Urbana is where your problems began, but I bet if you look back before Urbana—even years before—you'll find traces of a depressive tendency."

I did not have to search long for the memories, memories I'd overlooked in my efforts to explain the night. How had I failed before to connect the dots?

When I was eight, my family took a vacation with friends who owned a time-share many floors up in a beachfront high-rise, and I can remember standing on the balcony, peering through the iron railing, and wondering what it would feel like to fall, to throw myself off the edge. A swelling deep within was telling me to do it, and the temptation was both terrifying and exhilarating in the same instant. I was not an unhappy child, and I do not believe I wanted to die. But the compulsion to jump was real and intense, and I have wondered since if it was the first sign of the disturbed psyche that would overtake me four years later.

At age twelve, I slipped into severe sadness brought on by the move to junior high and to a new school where I knew almost no one. Making friends did not come naturally for me, and the whole year I was bullied mercilessly. Many afternoons, and then again at night, I cried myself to sleep from loneliness and ruined self-esteem. Two weeks before the end of the school year, I was suicidal. Alone in an empty house, I walked into the bathroom, opened the medicine cabinet, and thought, *I could swallow all of this and end it now.* But the will to live proved too much, and I sank instead to the floor in tears, heaving and convulsing next to the laundry hamper.

There were other times as well, in high school and early on in college, when I fell, without warning or cause, into shorter though no less profound spells of despondency, out of which no music or Scripture or reason could lift me. All I could do was lie on my bed, fighting back tears and waiting for the clouds to thin.

Once when this happened in college, I thought, *I must be homesick.* But I knew homesickness, and this was different. The heaviness lasted for days, pressing down on me till all I could do in between classes was sit in my room and cry. I remember friends were worried; one even came to my room and prayed for me. Then, as mysteriously as it had fallen, the sorrow lifted.

One year later I boarded a bus, headed for Urbana, Illinois, and the darkest night I had ever known.

Looking back, it is incredible I did not realize sooner that my problems preceded Urbana. People do not cry without reason. They do not randomly feel compelled to jump from balconies. And it is hardly normal for a twelve-year-old to stare into a medicine cabinet, contemplating suicide. Something was wrong long before Urbana. Yet even after realizing this clear and traceable depressive history, I could not let go of the spiritual connection my experience at Urbana demanded. The lights had gone out, this time, in worship. How could that be depression? And whatever the origin of this darkness, doubt had entered into it and my spirit was inexorably involved. I did not see how I could—or how any amount of medicine could ever make me—love a God who picks and chooses his children.

Brett Mitchell was having trouble trusting medical treatment as well. He wrote in an e-mail, "I just feel like I need so much more than any medicine or anything at all can do for me." Granted, Brett had, without his doctor's consent, taken himself off Paxil, and that had nearly pushed him over the edge. But he had stopped taking Paxil because he didn't feel it was working.

I asked Brett over the phone one night if he ever thought about suicide as a way out. "Yes," he said, "once a month on average, but quite a bit more the last few weeks. I know killing myself should not be an option, but sometimes the pain is just so bad that I want to die. What is the point of living if this is all there is?"

We were both reaching a point where we were out of new ideas for how to proceed. If medication was the answer, why had it not helped Brett? If prayer was the answer, why had it not helped either of us?

"There is nothing else for me to do," I said to Brett. "I've sought godly counsel, I've read all the right verses, and I've prayed about this from every angle possible. All I can do is wait."

There was one other thing I could do.

SEVEN

The Wisdom of Mentors

KRIS CARRAWAY HAD BEEN clear in her suspicion that my problem was primarily physical rather than spiritual, but I was concerned that her diagnosis was too heavily influenced by her own depressive past. Perhaps she had read too much of her story into mine. Before I could take the psychiatric route she suggested, I needed a second opinion.

Jeff Long, my pastor from back home, was, in true Southern Baptist fashion, a straight shooter, loyal to Scripture and blunt with his opinions. I was looking for such a man, one who would listen to my story, then look me in the eye and tell me the truth, even if it hurt. If Jeff thought I was lost, he would tell me. If he thought I was hardened in my heart against God, he would say so. The time for diplomacy was over. I didn't need tact; I needed raw, brutal honesty, and I knew Jeff would give it.

Jeff and I had met one other time, a year and a half earlier, shortly after Urbana. Our meeting hadn't helped much; at the time I was still uncertain how to articulate the tragedy, so Jeff didn't have a lot to go on. But he picked up enough from that one conversation to suspect a mood disorder.

"Do you struggle with depression?" he had asked after our discussion over lunch.

His question was now more relevant than ever, and I e-mailed a couple weeks before Thanksgiving of 1999 to ask if he could see me for a follow-up conversation when I was in town for the holiday.

We met in his office under the sanctuary, and for several minutes I filled Jeff in on all that had gone wrong since our last meeting, describing the despair in the starkest terms possible. Maybe I was trying to shock him, but if I was lost, I needed to know. If I was rejected by God, I wanted him to say it. I poured it all out, told him everything I had time for, then sat back in my chair, took a breath, and prepared myself for whatever Jeff would say.

"Do you want me to respond or just listen?"

I assured him I wanted his advice.

"Do you know or want to know where I fall on the issue of election?"

"I can probably guess," I said, "but yes, I want to know."

"I don't want to offend you, but I believe God chooses those he will save. When I was your age, people who believed in predestination made me so mad! But having now studied the Bible for years, I have come to accept it."

"But!" Jeff insisted, "That doctrine should be dealt with only when an individual is ready to wrestle"—a point he thought I wasn't at when I had first come upon Romans 9, or met Dawson and his disciples.

Jeff dealt so carefully with the subject of election that, even though I knew where he stood, I wasn't the least disturbed by anything he shared.

He continued, "Some things are not clear in the Bible for a couple of reasons. One, while they may be essential to the faith, they are not essential for our end of it. It is essential that God understand how predestination works because he is the one saving people. It is not essential that we understand it. Second, God has not revealed all there is to know about himself, but rather all we need to know for now. Learning to accept gray areas may be hard for our minds that think in terms of black and white, but it is necessary if we are going to honestly study the Bible."

Jeff added, however, that I needed to let the election issue go until I was in a better place to deal with it. "Election isn't the problem. You were having trouble months before you hit that wall."

His words sounded true, but the instruction would be hard to follow. I told Jeff that I felt guilty of fighting God, like I was resisting his will and whatever the truth was about predestination.

"No way," Jeff objected. "And I doubt God looks at it that way either."

Just the thought that God wasn't angry was helpful.

As we turned to the subject of my salvation, Jeff said he was sure—as sure as one can be of another person—that I was a Christian, that I would not have wrestled this long if my faith wasn't genuine. I would have, in his words, "punted and gone on to something else a long time ago," if I didn't truly believe.

At that, I relaxed a little. But if my problem wasn't election or insincere faith, was it a mood disorder? Jeff cautiously avoided any diagnoses that he wasn't qualified to make but said I obviously had a "propensity for depression." And he asked a piercing question, "Are you willing to live with depression the rest of your life if it means you will cling to God and remain humble in a way you never could if all was warm and fuzzy?"

> *I would not have wrestled this long if my faith wasn't genuine.*

Would I embrace this part of me as a gift from God rather than a curse? I could hardly stand the thought of battling my mutinous moods for a lifetime, and Kris Carraway had promised, after learning about my depression, that I would "never have to walk this way again." But what if I *would* have to?

In 2 Corinthians 12:7, the apostle Paul wrote, "To keep me from becoming conceited . . . there was given me a thorn in my flesh, a messenger of Satan, to torment me." We do not know the nature of Paul's thorn, but he says he begged God three times to take it away. The Lord's only response was, "My grace is sufficient."

Paul somehow, and perhaps only after much wrestling, reached a point where he could even thank God for his difficulty, and for the meekness it produced in his life. I was nowhere near giving thanks for my depression, but already I could see how it had humbled me.

Before the fear and darkness, I lacked compassion, and I dished out my theories on God's dealings with a confidence that bordered on arrogance. A confused friend from Campbell had asked me once how God could let people die and go to hell without ever hearing of Jesus. How was it fair that some had no access to the gospel while others were bathing in it? I shot her down with a quick, easy answer that I'd been fed by some book or Bible teacher. "Well, grace isn't fair," I said. "If it were fair, it wouldn't be grace. God isn't obligated to give anyone the truth. He would be fair in sending us all to hell. It is unfair that any of us goes to heaven."

How easily the answers rolled off my tongue when I was safe from the pain behind the questions. But the questions had gone from theoretical to personal, from academic to emotional, and all my simple logic now felt hollow and empty. Suffering had silenced my prideful tongue and knocked the swagger from my step. I was broken now, and my weakness made me understanding of others' failings. Was a lifetime of depression a price worth paying to remain humble before God? I didn't want to answer "yes" for fear I was signing up for such a life, but in my heart I had already agreed. Even if the dark night ended tomorrow, I never wanted to go back to my earlier manner of smug assurance about all God's ways. Yes, I would choose depression if it kept me humble.

Compassionate and level-headed in his thoughts, Jeff warned against assuming that anything he had to say was divinely inspired. "When people are desperate, they will take someone's advice as coming straight from God." So he encouraged me to keep working through my darkness, even if the process was messy: "You will plow through this, and it's okay to plow." With that, Jeff needed to head upstairs for the service, so we prayed and made our way to the sanctuary.

My head was abuzz with new wisdom. *I will plow through this, and it's okay to plow. God isn't angry at my confusion. Election isn't my problem. I would not have wrestled this long if my faith weren't genuine.*

After the service, Jeff smiled, gave me a hug and told me to keep in touch.

Brilliant. He was brilliant. He was honest about his view of election, confident in his advice, yet humble in his approach. I got no sense that Jeff had any agenda other than offering wise counsel, and I walked away feeling well-served by our time together.

* * *

I now had my second opinion. While Jeff was more hesitant than Kris to affix a label to my struggle, nothing he said contradicted Kris's belief that my darkness was more of the mind than of the soul. Both Jeff and Kris believed I was a genuine Christian. In fact, in the four years I was depressed, all but one of the people I asked—and I asked a lot of people!—said they were confident of my salvation. Only one refused to comment, saying it wasn't his place to make that call. Why did Jeff and Kris, and everyone else, think I was saved when the evidence associated with a life of faith seemed so absent from my life? Galatians 5:22-23 lists the fruit of the Spirit as love, joy, peace, patience, kindness, goodness, faithfulness, gentleness and self-control. You would have been hard-pressed to find any of those qualities in my life during the years of depression and doubt. But the fact that I *wanted* such fruit, and that I despised myself for the lack of it, only strengthened Kris's conviction that my brain was my enemy—a conviction she expressed in e-mails at the time:

EMAIL

Matt, you had a textbook conversion experience. You have evidenced a sincere desire to grow in your faith, to have fellowship, to get to know God better—not perfect, but sincere, open and honest. I have not yet heard anything that suggests you are secretly engaged in lifestyle choices that would sabotage or short-circuit the work of the Spirit of God in your life. We all do dumb things, give in to the flesh and have to ask God's forgiveness. Your walk has been very typical in that respect. But I see no evidence of heart-hardening, only genuine confusion and frustration over your freedom in Christ being more theoretical than experiential. So, if you are playing by the rules—and, "Try harder, slave!" is not one of them—why isn't your inheritance in Christ more real to you?

This is why I think your problem is emotional and not something that you can fix by willing it to go away. (I am climbing up on my medication soapbox again.) You are just having to work too hard to think positively and feel good about life. I know you are a serious guy, but you don't have to be a depressed guy.

Remember, too, that I was once sabotaged by my own mind. What I thought was logical, real and true, I saw later in retrospect–with a healthy mind–was twisted and skewed by bad chemistry. I continue to be amazed by the destructive messages my own brain was sending me. Yeah, yeah, yeah, I know Satan was having a heyday too, but he was getting unhindered cooperation from me, and I didn't even know it.

So there you have it. Bottom line, it's your call–until some doctor threatens to have you committed within two weeks like he did me. What a bad dream all that was.

Talk to you later. Pray for you much.

Kris

Kris never suggested that my suffering was *only* emotional, as if my soul were unaffected. She merely believed that the source of my trouble was my mind, not my spirit. But my deeply ingrained tendency toward black and white, one or the other thinking led me to interpret her advice as, "Choose one." I wrote back to suggest what must have seemed clear and apparent to Kris: What if my melancholy was the product of both chemistry *and* circumstance? Maybe I did lean toward dark moods; based on my history of depressive episodes, I could hardly argue otherwise. Could not that propensity, mixed with the doubts about God, have conspired to create the night? Kris responded:

*Makes perfect sense, Matt. When I was clinically depressed
there were some seriously depressing circumstances in my life
that were still there after the medication started helping
me think clearly. My environment didn't change, but I
changed. The very same circumstances that had driven
me to suicide before were now manageable—difficult, but
manageable. I didn't obsess anymore over negative things in
my life. I was able to see them for what they were and to do
what I could about them. The things I couldn't change I just
left alone and had real peace about them. It wasn't la-la land
and phony, fragile happiness. I didn't have to struggle to
convince myself to believe in God's goodness and grace—
I just believed. I hadn't got any more spiritual, but I no longer
felt angry at God or suspicious that he was getting perverse
pleasure out of destroying my life. . . All because medication
brought my brain chemistry back to normal. You're on the
right track, Matt.*

Kris

* * *

In addition to her advice that I see a doctor, Kris had been
encouraging me to join a church or college ministry. Though
I had been diligent in looking ever since I moved to Virginia,
I had yet to find a church with a thriving ministry for young
people just out of college, so I sat by myself in the pew most
Sundays, feeling very much alone and wishing for even a single friend. All I got, instead, was an hour of instruction about
things that I wanted to experience as true but could not.

"Turn your life over to God," one pastor said. "Watch what

he can do with it!" Nice sentiment. Very inspiring. I was sure I had given many people the same advice before the depression. But then there was me now. I would sing "Take My Life" and try to mean it, but nothing would happen. I'd pray at the altar and beg for God's mercy but get up feeling as cold and rotten as before.

One Sunday was particularly bitter. My mind had been seething all morning, and the music minister was bouncing up and down and grinning from ear to ear at the song in his heart as he led the church through hymn after hymn. I stood mumbling the lyrics and thinking, *If this guy gets any happier, he's going to float out the back door.*

The sermon that followed worship was, appropriately, on joy. "If our joy is missing," the preacher said, "something is separating us from God, and we should confess whatever it is and be restored." It all sounded so simple. Why wasn't it? We rose when the preacher was done, and I "joyfully" sang a few more songs before heading home, discouraged and alone. Sundays often ended this way.

Kris suggested I look to the university itself. Blacksburg is home to Virginia Tech, with many Christian groups on campus. "I'd love for you to check out Campus Crusade or Navigators or something similar," Kris said. "Walking folks like you through hard times is what they do for a living."

I learned of one ministry on campus that served the dual functions of church and student group, and I decided to give it a try. New Life Christian Fellowship, or NLCF, met on Sundays in the student center. The gathering was large—about six hundred students in the first of two morning services—and had a youthful vigor I'd not experienced elsewhere. The people were charged with desire, with love for God and for each other. I could see on their faces—young like mine, but happy—that they came willingly, not because of guilt or routine.

And there was vitality in their worship: eyes closed, heads bobbing to the beat and hands raised toward the ceiling in a seeming effort to touch the very face of God. It was not unlike Urbana. Only this time, I did not die in worship; after three years of this dark night, I was not expecting to love God or feel that he loved me. I went through the motions, singing the songs as best I could, omitting phrases and even whole verses if I thought my offering them would be an especial lie. And I experienced the usual envy as I looked around the room at the happy revelers, enjoying the presence of the One I'd lost three years earlier in a similar setting. But something was different about this envy. It was a hopeful jealousy, one that longed for what these people had. I thought, *If I just keep singing, keep coming week after week, maybe one day I'll be where they are.* And so I showed up every Sunday, singing in hopes that my worship would one day be sincere.

Often I came simply for the pastor's message. Something about the way J. R. Woodward spoke made me believe God might possibly love the whole world, not just his preselected few. *He might even love me.* I could not hold on to that faith beyond the sermon—the feeling faded when J. R. finished—but for a half hour each week, I could escape my anxious mind and sense something close to the peace I once knew.

I e-mailed the pastor one week to see if he would meet me for lunch; before I made NLCF my home, I wanted to know that its leaders could handle my confusion. J. R. and I met at a local Cajun restaurant on Main Street, and for the better part of an hour, he listened to my story.

J. R. was young, in his middle or late thirties, and quirky, not like any pastor I'd ever met. He fidgeted the whole meal yet seemed to catch every word I said. He wasn't nervous, just full of energy, and he could hardly sit still. At times he rested his right foot on the seat of his chair so that his knee was level with his chin. I had never seen anyone—certainly not a pastor—sit at a table like that. He was childlike in the way he seemed to lack any air of self-consciousness. And he was intent, absolutely engaged in what I was saying, even as he shifted positions in his seat. I got the feeling that this man loved meeting people and hearing their stories, even dark stories like mine. He was not put off by my doubts. While he did not, in that first encounter, offer any grand solutions to my troubles, he encouraged me, even inviting me to see a movie with him later in the week.

J. R. and the congregation of NLCF impressed me. They seemed genuine, following God with sincerity, loving each other like Jesus said to, and avoiding doctrinal hang-ups like mine. I wanted what these people had. I checked their statement of faith online for unorthodoxy and found them rock solid on the essentials, with plenty of breathing room in less important matters. If I was ever going to find God again, this seemed the most likely place in which I might do so.

I think I have found a church home.

Sundays and small group times with NLCF took the edge off my misery by confronting me with evidence that challenged my thinking. Before I found a church, I had been left to the devices of my failing mind, and the result was, in Kris's words, "unhindered cooperation" with the fog and fear and the cycles of rising and crashing. But now there was tangible evidence for cross-examination. If God did not love me, why did his people? Far from rejecting me, they had been inviting, leaving no doubt about their desire to see me incorporated into the fellowship of the church. Mike Swann, a full-time staff member with NLCF, met me at a local coffee shop across the street from the radio station where I worked and drove me to his home group for Bible study and worship. And he followed up with me to make sure I was finding my niche, making friends and feeling at home. The concern he and others showed took the edge off my pain, but the questions remained.

JOURNAL

MONDAY, FEBRUARY 14, 2000

Kris said in one of her e-mails, "What I thought was logical, real and true, I saw later in retrospect–with a healthy mind–was twisted and skewed by bad chemistry."

If our perception of truth is so heavily rooted in something as shallow as feelings, what does that say about our ability to ever be certain of the truth?

If depression had constructed, in part or in whole, this dark world in my mind where mountains seemed sinister and God could be evil—if bad feelings could do all of that, how could I trust the world constructed by good feelings? Maybe both worlds were merely reflections of mood with no basis in reality.

If our perception of truth is so heavily rooted in something as shallow as feelings, what does that say about our ability to ever be certain of the truth?

Of course, that argument was flawed, as was so much of my thinking at the time. The comparison was not between good feelings and bad, but between a healthy brain and one that was sick. If Kris was right, my mind was malfunctioning so that I could not rightly interpret either the physical or spiritual world around me as I would be able to if my brain were free of its disease.

I was beginning to consider that Kris could be right, that as real as the angry God in my head seemed, he might *only* be in my head, like a monster under a child's bed.

JOURNAL

TUESDAY, FEBRUARY 15, 2000

Maybe Jesus is not as I've imagined him. Maybe many things are not as they appear.

* * *

Springtime came to Blacksburg. Virginia Tech let out for
the semester, reducing NLCF to a few dozen lingering students and a handful of others who, like me, were not caught
up in the cyclical nature of a college town. The smaller congregation gave me opportunity to talk with leaders in the
church who were less busy after the school year. I saw myself
like the woman in the Gospels who pressed her way through
a crowd to touch the hem of Christ's robe. If I could work my
way through the crowd to these leaders—if I could just touch
these servants of God—maybe their faith could pass to me.

I knew that Jim Pace was a safe person to whom I could take
my questions. He was on staff with NLCF, and he'd also graduated from Virginia Tech with a degree in psychology. Based on
comments I'd overheard him make, I suspected Jim could offer
wisdom on both the mental and spiritual sides of my struggle.
But I had to press through the crowd to reach him.

Jim oversaw the follow-up team for NLCF. Every first-time
visitor, and every member who had requested help or information on one of the cards in the bulletins, would receive a visit
or phone call from someone on the team. I had the idea one
Sunday night to get near Jim by attending the follow-up meeting and feigning interest in helping out. I knew Jim would
ask me how I was doing. *That's just what ministers do.* When
he asked, I gave him a rehearsed "so-so" answer that subtly
implied I was in trouble.

"You going through a tough time?"

I vaguely mentioned something about predestination.

"You know," he said, and smiled understandingly, "that's

one of those issues that you wish God had just made clear in his Word."

What a relief to hear a full-time minister confess an incomplete knowledge of God and his will! Maybe there *was* a way to love God without answers to my questions. Could this man show me how?

"If there's ever anything I can do to help, let me know," Jim said. "You've been on my heart lately as I've been praying."

He's been praying for me! For weeks I had been asking God for a chance to talk with Jim, and all the while God had been talking to Jim about me. Hope and joy mingled together as I drove home from the follow-up meeting that night. Jim and I set a time and place to talk further, and on a Monday morning early in June, we met in a coffee shop downtown.

I was anxious as I entered and sat on the couch in front of Jim. I didn't know how I should explain everything, or even where to start. At first, I thought of limiting the time to an intellectual discussion of predestination, but Jim would have seen through that. He had been a psychology major, after all! He would have known my struggle was personal, so I told him everything.

Jim said many helpful things that day. He affirmed what so many others believed, that I was a Christian, that God was not my enemy and that something deeper was going on than just confusion over Romans 9. "A lot of people struggle to understand that passage," Jim said, "but they don't end up where you are. There's something else going on here, and I'd like to spend the summer getting at whatever that is." He suggested we meet once a week to talk, and said I should be prepared for this to take a while. "You didn't get into these wrong thought patterns overnight. It might take a couple years even to resolve these issues. But isn't it worth spending a couple years working this out so that you can have fifty years of basking in the love of God?"

I had been praying for a mentor like Jim, someone who would go the distance with me, who recognized that this hole I was in had been years in the making and that it might take as long to get out of it.

Echoing the apostle Paul in 2 Corinthians 1:4, Jim encouraged me to see the eventual fruit of all this, saying we can only give to others the comfort we have received from God: "Maybe God is preparing you for an encounter five or ten years down the road with a depressed Christian who is ready to throw in the towel on God, or even on life, and the only one who will be able to relate to him is you, Matt—because of this present struggle."

When our time was up, Jim closed the conversation with prayer. "God, raise Matt up from this to be a force for you like nothing the devil has ever seen."

JOURNAL

MONDAY JUNE 5, 2000

When I first met Kris Carraway at Trans World Radio, she could tell that I might be heading into a dark time in life. She suggested I find someone with whom I could be totally honest and who would not be shocked by the thoughts in my head.

Perhaps I have found him.

Jim and I began meeting weekly on Monday afternoons, and though I experienced no immediate breakthroughs, I received strong, consistent encouragement. My new mentor said he could see a day, on the other side of the confusion, when there would be a place for me on staff with NLCF. *Are you kidding?* I thought. *What kind of people do you hire?*

Jim believed that too much focus on the sternness of God and too little attention to his kindness—Romans 11:22 said to consider both—had created space for Satan to corrupt my confidence in God's love for me. The thought of God choosing his people, therefore, brought fear rather than gratitude. A more balanced theology, even if for a while it felt forced and untrue, would likely bring peace.

Jim set a deadline: "If by the end of the summer we've been unable to crack this thing, I want you to see a Christian counselor."

What I liked about Jim's approach was that everything was on the table—counseling, medication, prayer and fasting—and no avenue was given more weight than another. All were valid and potential paths to healing.

Was there, however, any reason to hope? It had been so long, and the climb toward freedom seemed impossibly steep. But Jim believed, and that helped me believe.

The summer would be the test.

EIGHT . . .

Signs of Light

HEALING CAME SLOWLY, LIKE a sunrise, a gradual moving from darkness to dawn. One bleeds into the other, night into day, so that you cannot say where one ended and the other began. All you know is that light has come. So it was with my release.

SUNDAY, JULY 2, 2000

When I think back to those first days, to the depression, the fear, the hopelessness, wondering how I would make it through a single day, dangerously close to a complete breakdown–just to see where I am now leads me to thanksgiving and awe.

And none of my questions are answered. But I've seen enough to think this must be part of God's plan for me, "plans for welfare, and not calamity, plans to give me a future and a hope" (Jeremiah 29:11).

The first signs of light came during the spring semester that I joined NLCF, a few months before Jim and I began meeting. I did not notice at the time these subtle shifts in thought and mood, but reviewing my journals, on the other side of darkness, I can see now the slow progression.

* * *

It is hard to know, after *Life Is Beautiful,* why I agreed to watch another film about the Holocaust. Jason Butler drove in from Pearisburg for the evening, and we rented a movie because it was cheap entertainment, somehow settling on *Schindler's List.* Perhaps I was afraid to *not* watch it, afraid of what that meant.

C. S. Lewis said, "Reality, looked at steadily, is unbearable," and I suspect that is why many people never look at it at all. I never wanted to be that kind of person, shielding myself from truth because it would hurt. I probably agreed to *Schindler's List* for the same reason I forced myself at times to listen to preachers who were strong on God's sovereignty, even though I knew the fear and falling those decisions would bring: I was afraid that, by not watching or listening, maybe I was hiding my face from reality and rejecting whatever was true.

> *If I hid my face from what hurt and if I made God into whatever image I wanted, my solace would be an illusion.*

Any healing, for me, would've been empty if it came by submerging myself in fantasy until the pangs of reality had faded beyond feeling. If I hid my face from what hurt and if I made God into whatever image I wanted, my solace would be an illusion. I would have to face the dark night again, sometime later, once the illusion wore thin. I never wanted to go through this again. Whoever God was and whatever the truth was, I wanted to face it and make my peace with it now.

> And I waited. Waited for the scenes I knew would come, the images that would whisper in my ear again the old blasphemies of an evil God. . . . The awful images came. . . . The blasphemies never did.

Jason and I kicked back on the couch my parents had given me and started the movie, pausing as needed to up the volume on the TV whenever my aircraft-for-an-air-conditioner roared into service and took flight. And I waited. Waited for the scenes I knew would come, the images that would whisper in my ear again the old blasphemies of an evil God. I waited for the mound of murdered Jews, naked and stacked one on top of the other.

The awful images came. The blasphemies never did.

I watched that lifeless mound of Jews burn before me; I took the image into me, processed it, felt the evil of it—but I did not crash. No abyss. No falling. And no questions. I knew God had seen the horror. I knew he had allowed it for reasons completely beyond me. I knew he could have stopped it if he had wanted to. But none of this seemed to evidence an evil

God. Why? What was different now from two years earlier in that theater in Charlotte? The Holocaust was just as wicked now, and God appeared every bit as silent in the face of it. I wasn't numb to the thought of it all, and I wasn't holding back the accusations. I should have been sinking again into the pit, but I wasn't. The movie ended, the credits rolled, and I stood up feeling very much as I had hours earlier.

Jason was spending the night on my couch to avoid his sister's slumber party back home, and once he was asleep, I reached for my journal and set down a few thoughts on the evening before heading off to sleep myself. I quoted Psalm 145:8-9, "The Lord is gracious and compassionate, / slow to anger and rich in love. / The Lord is good to all; / he has compassion on all he has made."

"It will take a miracle to set my heart free," I wrote, "but God's character keeps me asking and hoping."

What was the source of this new hope? What had caused it? The character of God, which seemed so much in question after *Life Is Beautiful,* was somehow firmly intact after *Schindler's List.* I had gone from abhorring God's nature to hoping in it, and none of my circumstances had changed.

I thought about what Kris had said: "What I thought was logical, real and true, I saw later in retrospect—with a healthy mind—was twisted and skewed by bad chemistry." Could it be that simple?

In *Disappointment with God,* Philip Yancey wrote, "Saints become saints by somehow hanging on to the stubborn conviction that things are not as they appear." Had I subconsciously been hanging on for years to that "stubborn conviction" buried deep inside me? Had all the questions, which had been so in the forefront of my mind, covered over but not smothered the seed of faith that was struggling to bring its fruit to the surface?

Yancey said, "Job saw the darkest side of life, heard the deepest silence of God, and still believed."

Maybe that was me. Maybe things were not as they appeared.

* * *

Inspired by Job's climactic meeting with God in the whirlwind, I had always hoped for a similarly breathtaking and instantaneous rescue from the dark night. I wanted a quick antidote that I could point others to and say, *"This* is how God saved me!" I wanted to offer others the same path to freedom I had taken, which only seemed possible if I were fixed in a flash.

But, in the end, my healing was much more gradual. Like C. S. Lewis emerging from grief after his wife's death, "There was no sudden, striking, and emotional transition. Like the warming of a room or the coming of daylight. When you first notice them they have already been going on for some time." I only know that, day by day, the mountains seemed less sinister, and the world not so hopeless.

I had been, in my depression, like a man wearing sunglasses. I saw the world as darker than it really was. And eventually—I don't know when I reached the point—I had worn the glasses long enough that I forgot I had them on. I began to think I was seeing the world as it was, when in fact everything was dimmed by the darkened lenses through which I viewed all of life. I knew I was getting better when I remembered the glasses, when rays of unfiltered light broke through, reminding me that I was seeing through a glass darkly.

The clouds had lingered long enough that I had come to truly believe my twisted, cynical view of life—where everyone was only evil all the time and where there was no reason to hope for any good in this world. But I remember the moment, standing in the on-air studio at the radio station, when a single ray of light broke through. I thought, *Is that really possible? Is it at all reasonable to think that I've discovered "the truth" about life and that everyone else is deceived to be so happy?* It was only a thought, a solitary ray, but it was the beginning. In time, the glasses came off, and I saw again the world unfiltered.

The healing process was shaky at first. The good times were genuinely good, but they were laced with the frustration of knowing they wouldn't last. If I read a certain verse of Scripture or heard a preacher mention predestination—or if I just woke up wrong—I would crash again. The happy days were a walk on thin ice. I was being held up, but not by much.

God, let it hold this time! Let the good days last.

The foundation cracked beneath me as I tried stepping lightly, hoping to avoid the weak spots, the triggers that would bring back the fear and darkness; one wrong step and the ice would break and I would sink into cold despair. I ran through this cycle repeatedly until one time the ice just didn't break.

For months, the fear of relapse hung over the healing,

threatening a new storm, but the healing held, and grew, spurred on by a steady intake of grace and truth from my mentors. Those Monday meetings with Jim Pace must have tested his faith when, after weeks of repeating himself, he saw no change in me. All of his encouragement appeared to be bouncing off. But beneath the surface, just out of sight, a tiny seed was being nourished.

The clear, cool logic of Kris Carraway was another assault on my melancholy, and I believe in time the force of her motherly wisdom broke through the fog. I was mentally sick. Perhaps the spiritual was mixed up in it as well, and Jim was working with me to address it, but there was something physically, fearfully wrong with my brain.

In one of her many e-mail petitions that I seek medical help, Kris said,

I can't help thinking that if you were a woman, with hormonal ups and downs, you might better understand how body chemistry can sabotage even the feeling or sensory experience of the fruit of the Spirit. When the body and mind are in sync with our spirit, yes, very real and valid feelings of peace and joy and all the other fruit can be felt. But throw in a migraine or PMS or bad brain chemistry or a chemo treatment for cancer or a diabetic sugar low . . . you get the picture.

I never received clinical help for the depression because the fog began lifting before I could reach a decision about taking medicine. But doubtless, Kris was right. The disease was indeed more of the mind than of the soul, and I likely prolonged my suffering needlessly when help was within reach. Medicine helped Brett Mitchell. It was not a silver bullet, certainly—counseling was, as it usually is, also necessary—but antidepressants were a factor in Brett's finding peace. Might they have been for me as well, had I followed Brett's lead and seen a doctor?

I suspect my hesitations concerning psychiatry were due, in part, to a faulty understanding of human nature. I had been taught, through books and sermons and Sunday school lessons, that we are primarily spiritual beings. We have bodies which help us get around, but which are mostly ancillary to life. People are, at their core—or so the teaching goes— priceless souls in unimportant shells.

A cloudy, melancholic mind rendered me incapable of seeing how foreign this belief is to the faith as defined in Scripture; Jesus' living, dying and rising in the body is essential to Christianity. But it sounds lofty to say we are mostly spiritual beings, and so I consistently, time and again, downplayed the physical aspects of my sickness and elevated the spiritual. Medication was, thus, irrelevant at best, a dangerous distraction at worst.

I am thankful Brett knew better, that he didn't give up on medication when Paxil seemed ineffectual. He asked for and received from his counselor a referral to a psychiatrist. Brett had begun to suspect that his problem was not that medication was the wrong answer but that his family doctor did not know *which* medication to prescribe. There were dozens of antidepressants on the market, and Brett decided he needed a specialist in the field to pinpoint a particular drug for him to try. Through painful, yet patient, trial and error, Brett found medicine that, in conjunction with regular counseling, helped burn away the fog.

By never seeking professional help, I missed out on much I might have learned firsthand, through sessions with a counselor or psychologist, about the causes of my darkness. I missed the chance to see by experience what the medical field has done to alleviate the bitter pain of depression. And I took terrible risks with

> *The disease was indeed more of the mind than of the soul, and I likely prolonged my suffering needlessly when help was within reach.*

my life. The threat of hell had kept me off the path to suicide. But suppose that threat had lifted. Or that my suffering had grown to a point where hell, by comparison, appeared merciful. Might I have then joined the roughly 30,000 who, each year, end their tormented lives? My stubborn refusal to heed Kris's advice looks, a decade later, very unwise indeed.

I did manage to make a couple good decisions during my depression. First, I did not keep my suffering hidden. I let people in. Not everyone, of course, but enough people to ensure I was receiving some counsel. And I did not withdraw from those around me who cared. One typical and particularly insidious effect of the disease is the temptation to shrink from all social contact. A simple conversation, pleasurable to a healthy mind, is utterly exhausting to one that is ill. Afflicted souls, therefore, retreat from what could be (and what was for me) a wonderful source of hope: the community of saints.

NLCF, my church, became a place where I could dream: If these people could love God and follow him with joy—if they could worship with a smile despite their many questions about God—maybe, one day, I could as well. And they wanted me to. They wanted me to know their God. In so many little ways, nothing flashy or grand—an encouraging word from Eric, a smile and a hug from Sara, an invitation to dinner at Brad's—they held out hope for me and welcomed me into their family. Over time, these simple expressions of Christ warmed my heart and mind to the thought of a truly good Lord. Even when they did not know what to say, or how specifically they might help, these normal, healthy believers gave me a goal, an example of who I might become.

And they cheered me on toward that goal. Long before I was ready, before many churches would have given me the chance, Jim Pace asked me to help plan and implement a weekly small group Bible study. There were conditions, of course. If any matters came up in the discussion that touched on my confusion, I had to defer to him or to someone in the group with a steadier faith than mine. We were just going to try this plan out for a while, just going to see if it could work. No promises. What a bold, faith-filled risk he took on me!

It was just the thing I needed. Soon I saw good fruit coming from my soul, which for four years had produced only rottenness. Members of the group affirmed me in this new role, telling me how they grew from what I had to share each week. This was strong medicine for my battle-scarred mind: *If God would use me for good in the lives of others, might he not also desire blessing for me?*

I made wonderful friends in that small group. A couple of them, two brothers, Chris and Tim, invited me to leave my dark, dismal hole of a home and move in with them. Our new apartment was similarly drab, sunk almost entirely in the ground with only a sliver of window to let in any light. One might question this self-interment: What wisdom prompts a depressed man, obsessed with thoughts of death and burial, to make his home in the dirt? But I was moving in with friends, out of aloneness and into community.

A year later, I moved again, to another apartment with two more friends, Ross and John. Their penchant for humor, for laughter and fun, lifted me out of many bleak moods, and the memories of that time, some of them hysterical, are with me forever.

It would take a lifetime to thank the many people at NLCF who went about the ordinary business of life with such contagious, godly zest that I could not help but eventually catch what they had. I had wished for a sudden, dramatic rescue— God in a whirlwind—to come and set me free. Instead, I largely owe my healing to a more subtle God, working gradually through the persistent love of his people.

Oswald Chambers said after his own four-year dark night, "Nothing but the overruling grace of God and the kindness of friends kept me out of an asylum." I too owe my sanity, in part, to friends who stayed with me through the darkness and walked me out of it, though at times this must have been a hard service. I can never repay the debt, but I am forever grateful for their efforts; they were not in vain.

The strength of this love, and the healing it brought me, was greatly tested in 2001 when my friend Baker Falls fell suddenly and gravely ill. Baker had been with me on the worst night of my life, his smile having saved me from despair after *Life Is Beautiful*. Baker was preparing for mission work in Africa when, the night before he was to fly out of the U.S., he entered a hospital with a high fever he couldn't shake. He soon learned he had leukemia. Throughout his sickness, which dragged on for months, Baker never quit laughing, never lost faith. And he never surrendered his trademark smile. He was the same when sick as when well, faithfully following Jesus to the end.

Baker Falls died on March 6, 2002, leaving behind a beautiful example of how to cling to faith in the worst of times. That example, combined with the love of so many from my church, kept me from falling again.

The healing held. Much like a sunrise, the darkness of my heart had slowly given way to light, and when my mind was at last stable enough to deal constructively with my questions, I turned to the task of unraveling the theological aspects of my long, dark night.

IT WAS NOT ENOUGH to simply feel better. I was looking for the God I had lost four years earlier. The black moods had abated, but the coinciding doubts lingered. If I was to find a lasting peace, I would need some resolution to my many questions and to the paralyzing suspicion that perhaps the Good News was not so good after all.

Four years of conflicting preaching, picked up here and there from visiting churches or listening to the radio, had killed any confidence I had that I might ever lay hold of the one, true God. I heard one teacher, during my depression, say, "God doesn't save people because he loves them; he saves them for his glory!" I did not know what the man meant or if he had ever read John 3:16, but my troubled soul, so skeptical of God's concern for me, took this pastor's sermon as further evidence I might be damned: If God saves some for his glory, perhaps he refuses to save others for the same reason.

This and a thousand other comments made in passing by well-meaning preachers had been caught in the confused web that was my mind and were summarily twisted into a grotesque, contorted caricature of God. Separating fact from fiction, truth from untruth, would be a tricky but necessary process.

Was God evil? Was he, in Kris's words, "getting perverse pleasure out of destroying my life"? The feeling that he might be was very real. Yet, even in my most desperate moments, I had only just been able to entertain the idea; I could never quite embrace it. In the light of a healthy brain, I could see that the idea itself was a product of the emotional anguish I was then enduring.

But how could a God who chooses some for salvation and others for torment be, by any reasonable definition of the word, good? I was stuck on that question. Even before the clouds retreated, I rejected the possibility of total human free will. If people were always free in every circumstance to choose their course, then human beings would have ultimate control of the world. The title Lord, as applied to God, would be honorary at best. The Sovereign would find himself in the awkward position of hoping his creation fulfilled his purpose but being wholly impotent to make it happen. This seemed to contradict everything I had read in Scripture.

I thought I would, at last, have to cast my lots with Adam Dawson and pray that in time I could learn to love a God who chooses some and hates the rest. And for a long time I did try, asking God sincerely that he make me believe in total predestination if it were true. I would not decide against Adam's view for emotional reasons. In the face of horrible mental torment, I would still have preferred truth with suffering to happiness with a lie.

But try as I might to force the issue, I could not reconcile Adam's teaching with Scripture either. His entire doctrine hung on the belief that God had selected some for bliss and had rejected the rest, consigning them by default to everlasting pain. But John 3:16 says, "God so loved the world"—the whole world, not certain people in it. And love in Scripture, much more than a feeling, is a determination to seek the good of others, even at great cost to oneself: "he *gave* his one and only Son."

The Bible goes one step further still, stating that God is more than simply motivated by love; according to 1 John 4:8, "God *is* love." Surely then he could not violate his own nature. If there is even one person God does not want to save, wouldn't it be a fair conclusion to say that God does not love that person and that, however loving God might be, he is not love itself?

Adam would (and did) argue that damning some was necessary to glorify God's justice and wrath in a way not possible if God set out to save us all. That made sense to me but failed to answer one nagging question: No matter how right God might be in choosing some but not others, how could he deny the essence of his being—which, again, is love—in order to do so?

If I dismissed both extremes as scripturally untenable, I would have to find some third alternative, but all I had heard was that it was either total sovereignty or total free will. Accepting some blend of the two would involve a bit of stretching on my part. I was a highly structured thinker, and I liked my theology black and white, systematic and easily explained. But what could I do when Scripture seemed to support both positions?

I saw Jesus in the Gospels, weeping over the city, crying, "O Jerusalem, Jerusalem, you who kill the prophets and stone those sent to you, how often I have longed to gather your children together, as a hen gathers her chicks under her wings, but you were not willing!" (Matthew 23:37). Not willing? Couldn't he have made them? Why would a sovereign Savior ever need to weep over his creatures not doing what they were predestined to do? Moreover, why would he weep for their rejection when he had ordained it? It didn't wash. But then Paul says bluntly in Romans 9:18, that, "God has mercy on whom he wants to have mercy, and he hardens whom he wants to harden." I even found one place, Acts 13, where the two doctrines stood side by side:

> *The longer I stared at the problem, the more suspicious I grew of extremes in either direction.*

Then Paul and Barnabas answered them boldly: "We had to speak the word of God to you first. Since you reject it and do not consider yourselves worthy of eternal life, we now turn to the Gentiles. For this is what the Lord has commanded us:

"'I have made you a light for the Gentiles,
that you may bring salvation to the ends of the earth.'"
When the Gentiles heard this, they were glad and
honored the word of the Lord; and all who were appointed
for eternal life believed.

The Jews freely rejected salvation—no hardening from God implied—but the Gentiles were chosen by God for it. Verse 46 was a free-will delight. Then, just two verses later, a celebration of sovereignty. How was I supposed to reconcile this? The longer I stared at the problem, the more suspicious I grew of extremes in either direction.

For four years my devastated mind had tried and failed to make sense of how intelligent people, reading the same texts, could paint perfectly opposing pictures of God. I would hear Adam Dawson at Campbell teach, with Scripture to support his claim, that God loves only the elect. Then I'd hear my pastor on Sunday preach from the same Bible that God desires to save all. The confusion was incredible. *Would the real God please stand up?*

> *As the haze burned off I could see that Scripture portrayed God as both gracious and severe, that one perspective minus the other was a distortion.*

But with the sunrise had come clarity of mind, and as the haze burned off I could see that Scripture portrayed God as both gracious and severe, that one perspective minus the other was a distortion. I could also see that, almost without exception, the total-free-will advocates were drawn to the gentle, merciful Savior, and they displayed those attributes in their own lives, while the adherents to total sovereignty were attracted to, and reflected most strongly, a holy God of justice. I began to wonder what role personality plays in leading us to stake out either position. Could these doctrinal extremes be more a construct of temperament than of truth?

Maybe this is why the apostle Paul refers to the church as a body, a single unit consisting of many varied, but equally important, parts. Maybe God is too big, too rich, to be displayed by one person, and Paul knew it. We need each other, the parts together as a whole, to even approach a complete picture. We might be looking at the same Jesus, but picking up and then projecting only those aspects of him that our individual tendencies highlight. Maybe this was true of the biblical writers as well; maybe that's why we have four Gospel accounts instead of one, or why the letter James wrote sounds so different from those of Paul. And, perhaps, because the biblical writers were varied in their personalities, I found a tension in Scripture between human responsibility and divine sovereignty—one I wasn't meant to resolve.

My rational mind, so in love with neatly-packaged, clearly-defined theology, was eventually drawn to a painful admission, one I would have escaped if there had been another way: in this matter, God's ways were simply a mystery. *A mystery!* Was I allowed to believe in such a thing? Four years in an academic environment left me thinking that God could be dissected, studied and fully understood. It was almost a maxim in that culture that we know God by explaining him, and I had followed that maxim faithfully beyond my Campbell days. *Had God warned me long ago of the danger in such a view?* I remembered the Tozer book my friend Charlie had given me and how I'd strangely flipped it open to page 64.

God will not hold us responsible to understand the mysteries of election, predestination and the divine sovereignty. The best and safest way to deal with these truths is to raise our eyes to God and in deepest reverence say, "O Lord, Thou knowest." Those things belong to the deep and mysterious profound of God's omniscience. Prying into them may make theologians, but it will never make saints.

"The deep and mysterious profound." The mysteries!

And had I followed Romans far enough, past chapters 9 and 10, and into 11, I would have found the apostle Paul, in verse 33, reaching the same conclusion, as if he'd stumped himself with his discourse on God's saving ways: "Oh, the depth of the riches of the wisdom and knowledge of God! / How unsearchable his judgments, / and his paths beyond tracing out!"

Mystery was now a means of worship. I was suddenly opened to the possibility of exulting in a God bigger than my laundry list of doctrines. He was alive, and vibrant, and massive! He defied my explanations and became more knowable the less familiar he seemed. This was the God who inhabits the heavens, a God substantial enough to both create the stars and abide in my heart. How could he be easily defined? How could my finite mind fully comprehend the Infinite?

I began to sing to God once more.

> *Holy, You are still holy*
> *Even though I don't understand Your ways*
> *And sovereign, You will be sovereign*
> *Even when my circumstances don't change*

Worship was wrestling, a way of fighting off the darkness and preventing a relapse. Happy songs of praise were still hard for me to hear, but I found a few songs of struggle in the radio station's music library that I could offer to God honestly.

In the evenings after work, I would get on my knees next to the CD player in my bedroom, and I would do battle for my faith, singing "You Are Still Holy" over and over, and often through tears.

> *Holy, You are still holy*
> *Even when the darkness surrounds my life*
> *And sovereign, You will be sovereign*
> *Even when confusion has blinded my eyes*

Aaron Tate, of the group Caedmon's Call, was so careful with his words that he would sometimes spend a year crafting a single song, and his lyrics became prayers to God from me during the early days of sunrise.

> *Sometimes I fear maybe I'm not chosen*
> *You've hardened my heart like Pharaoh*

And that would explain why life is so hard for me
And I am sad Esau hated
Crying against what's fated
Saying Father, please, is there any left for me
Cast out my doubts, please prove me wrong
'Cause these demons can be so headstrong

I played "Prove Me Wrong" for Jim Pace one afternoon as we drove around Blacksburg running errands. He remarked, "Matt, I've heard songs before that dealt with your issues, but I've never heard a song that was line for line everything you're going through."

Listening to Aaron Tate was like finding a brother I never knew I had. Someone understood me. Among the most difficult aspects of the dark night was the sense of isolation, the terrible suspicion that no one else in the world had felt my pain. I knew people had asked the same questions, but I had never met another person so tormented by the implications of those questions: *What if I'm not chosen? What if all my tears will not change what is fated?* Aaron Tate understood, and I was not alone.

In time, and after much healing, I was able to embrace the mystery of predestination. I settled on the most humble position I could think of, one that acknowledged my ignorance of God's ways and that refused to malign anyone else's viewpoint. (Adam Dawson was still my brother, and there was always the chance that he was right.) Whenever people would ask what I believed about the subject, I would tell them I thought the two perspectives were somehow in harmony so that we both choose God and are chosen by him. I had no idea how that worked, of course, but I was finally at peace about it.

My faith in God's ultimate rule over the universe was stronger for all the questions I asked, a much richer faith for having come through the darkness, and one that did not need to insult mystery by calling it contradiction. C. S. Lewis said, "Heaven will solve our problems, but not, I think, by showing us subtle reconciliations between all our apparently contradictory notions. The notions will all be knocked from under our feet. We shall see that there never was any problem."

If I could not solve the issue of election, I at least needed to settle the central question of my faith: *Am I saved?* I could not rest as long as I had doubts about the condition of my soul. Where was the line between mere mental ascent and genuine heart commitment to my beliefs? If, for the disciples, believing in Jesus meant leaving their nets and following Christ quite literally, how could I know I had abandoned all to go after him? If I had, why was my heart empty, devoid of any feelings of love for Jesus that would seem to be the obvious fruit of authentic faith in him?

I had something close to a breakthrough one night while talking to Eric Stenborg, a friend from church. After listening to me describe my situation, Eric thought for a second, then said, "Either there is something really wrong with me, and I don't know it, or there is something really *not* wrong with you, and you don't know it, because what you just described pretty much fits my own experience with God."

I had just laid out what I thought was a good case for why

I might not be a Christian, listing my every wrong desire and bad motive so that it was clear how evil my heart was. But rather than convincing Eric of my depravity, I more convinced him that I was normal, with spiritual high times and low times like anyone else. Could it be that I had so analyzed my heart, spying out every hint of sin, and was so focused on the evidence that might condemn me, that I had forgotten to look for signs of faith as well? Maybe others saw a more accurate picture of me by considering all the facts, instead of looking only at the pieces that supported the theory I had already decided was probably true.

But, *What if they are wrong? What if the uncertainty I feel is the Holy Spirit's work, making me uneasy about the condition of my soul?* As the clouds of depression cleared away, however, I could see the hole in this logic. Conviction from God should lead to repentance and relief. The guilt I felt left me in perpetual doubt, never moving me to a better place. In retrospect I wish I had kept a count of how many times I went down to the front of a church during an altar call, hoping this would be the time God would hear my cries. I got up feeling saved every time, but the emotions never lasted the day. If my need had been for God's pardon, he would have given it the first time I asked. Romans 10:13 says it's as simple as calling out to God, "For, 'Everyone who calls on the name of the Lord will be saved.'" I should not have needed to keep begging, and the fact that the begging brought no freedom meant that my need was for something other than salvation. It did not mean God had rejected me but that he had already given what I was asking for. Slowly, I surrendered to reason: my anxiety, like so much of my struggle, had been the result of an unhealthy brain.

From this I learned one of the most important lessons of the dark night, that peace with God, as with love for him, is more than a feeling. When Romans 5:1 says we have "peace with God" because of faith in the sacrifice of Christ, it is not talking about a sensory experience. Peace here is the condition in which we who have believed find ourselves: the war is over. The peace treaty is signed, and we who once were enemies of God are now even more than his allies. We are sons and daughter of God, and family, brothers and sisters, to one another. The old grievances are forgotten, and all the wrath meant for us has been expended on Christ at the cross. God has nothing but good intentions toward us. The relationship is secure. *This* is peace. Not the flimsy, inconsistent feelings that ebb and flow with the ups and downs of our physiology and our circumstances. Emotions are a gift, but I learned in the dark that we must be careful of the conclusions we let them draw for us.

This peace, when rightly understood, brought a final, lasting healing to my mind. The dark night had ended, though a couple of questions still remained.

TEN . . .

After the Storm

I HAVE NEVER BEEN back to that dank little theater in Charlotte, though I did drive past it once. Years after that desperate December night, and after I had come through the depression, I went looking for the place where I hit bottom. I searched online and drove all over Charlotte, but to no avail. *Maybe they tore it down,* I thought. This seemed a just fate after what had happened there.

Then one day, and quite by accident—if there are, in fact, accidents—I found it. Leaving a hospital where I had been visiting a friend, I took a wrong turn and drove right past the theater. The Starbucks next door gave it away.

I could have wrecked twice in that moment, once from simply, and finally, finding the place, and then from reading the address: 607 Providence Road.

Providence! I could only laugh at the sheer improbability. *Of all the streets in Charlotte . . .*

The Manor Theater appeared much the same to me from

the outside as I remembered it from a decade earlier. I hear it's been remodeled inside—though, again, I haven't been.

I have, likewise, never been back to Urbana, Illinois. How would it look now in the light of a healthy mind? What would I feel to walk inside Assembly Hall? Perhaps someday I'll plan a road trip there (though never again in the drear of December).

I've spent a decade asking the questions from that time in my life. Mostly I'm at peace with what I've gathered. Ten years later, however, I still wonder two things: *What caused the darkness, and why did God allow it?*

Author, physician and psychiatrist Dwight L. Carlson suggests that many cases of mental illness have, as their root, "a combination of nature, nurture and choice." A genetic predisposition, mixed with childhood trauma and poor life decisions, can cause depression and other psychological sicknesses. Whether this was true of me is difficult to know. I do find some evidence of mental illness in my family tree—a distant relative, generations back, committed suicide after several attempts and a long war with depression. But, since emotional problems are often hidden, I cannot tell how rampant they might run in my ancestry.

My experience growing up was, I would say, mostly normal. The transition to middle school was awful, but it is for many kids who never contemplate suicide. And life in college was unfolding well around the time I started sinking. I had adapted quickly to university life: made good friends and good grades; joined a local church; served in various ministries on campus; avoided the moral traps college life offers.

I cannot point to anything about the transition that should have led to a fall.

I *can,* however, point to bad choices I made that, while not initiating my illness, certainly prolonged and possibly worsened it. Once night fell, I persisted to the end in seeking a spiritual cause to an emotional problem, despite several older, very trustworthy saints suggesting I might be on the wrong track. I never saw a doctor, which should have been my first step. Many medical conditions can cause depressive symptoms. Had my moods been ruled the source, not merely the symptoms, of my problem, I could have moved on to treatment for clinical depression, which might have cut the dark night from four years to mere months.

None of this, however, explains the role Urbana played in my swift descent. I have conceded the fact that, as Kris Carraway believed, my problems did not begin at Urbana, that my mind was beginning to fail long before I boarded that bus. And I'm not at all sure anymore that God intended for Ima to hand me that check for $350 so that I would attend the conference; likely, I read too much into my circumstances at the time. Nonetheless, what was it about a moment of worship that caused my world to suddenly crumble? Perhaps the clouds had been gathering for months, but the light went out in an instant. Why?

After ten years, I have accepted that I may never know, as I may also never know why God permitted it. I believe he is sovereign (however that works). He who can see the end from the beginning saw the fog and confusion into which I would slip in the aftermath of Urbana. He saw the four years of fear and darkness, the threat of hell I would live under every day. And for reasons unclear to me, he permitted it.

Perhaps it simply needed to be, a part of my discipleship. God says he opposes the proud but gives grace to the humble; maybe the devastation was a severe but necessary mercy. Still I ask, *Why?* And did I learn from the darkness everything God intended? Did I squander any of my pain?

> *I will have to relinquish my demands to know why to a God who does not always explain himself, and to trust that the end will be worth it.*

The Bible does not say when, or if, Job learned of the wager in heaven between God and the devil. Job may never have known what precipitated his disaster. Maybe knowing would have destroyed the good work going on in him. Whatever the reason, Job likely lived, as I have had to live, without a full understanding of the tragedy endured. I imagine making peace with that fact was difficult for Job, as it has been for me.

Life will be this way sometimes. I will have to relinquish my demands to know why to a God who does not always explain himself, and to trust that the end will be worth it. Like Job, I must confess, "I know that You can do everything, / and that no purpose of *Yours* can be withheld from You" (Job 42:2 NKJV). I must believe God's purpose is good, however great the mystery.

Perhaps a partial answer to my *why* can be found, not in the storm itself, but in everything that followed. I discovered in the aftermath, once the clouds scattered and the sun returned, that I was no longer the judgmental man of my early faith. In the night, I had learned a deep compassion and grace for those who struggle. My heart now hurt for hurting people, and it did not take them long to find me.

A year into the healing, and shortly after I started leading a small group for NLCF, a college student showed up at my door late on a Wednesday night, his wrists slit by a razor in a failed suicide attempt. He had cut himself an hour earlier and held his arms underwater in his bathtub to keep the wounds from clotting. Only a timely call from his mother had shaken his will to die. He stood at my door trembling, incoherent and ghost-white from the loss of blood.

My pastor, J. R. Woodward, came over, and we got a little food into the student and dressed his wounds—by then the bleeding had stopped. In the morning, we would drive to St. Albans mental hospital in the neighboring town of Radford.

I was awake the whole night, listening for the young man as he slept restlessly, and as the hours passed, I never once asked myself how anyone could want to die. I knew how. I remembered. And on the way to St. Albans I could only think, *I'm finally going to a mental hospital, but not for me.*

This was my introduction into ministry and an early sign of what shape that ministry would take. The student was out of the hospital in a few days, and he recovered from his dark night over time, but he was only the first of many desolate souls I encountered as the years went by. I felt that God was bringing them to me, a steady stream of, most often, college students looking for anyone who understood their pain. Increasingly my heart was with them and less in my work at the radio station.

Jim Pace had told me in our first Monday morning meeting during the summer of my healing, that once I was past the night there would be a place for me on staff. I hardly believed him. *What kind of people do you hire?* But by 2003, that place had opened, and I stepped into full-time ministry with NLCF.

The steady stream continued. One student wrote to me after a Sunday service on campus,

EMAIL

Why do I feel like this? Why can't I just get it? If God exists, then why can't I feel him?

I stare at everybody in church, as they write notes about the talk or reach toward the ceiling in worship, and I just wonder what's going on in their heads? Do they actually believe this? I really have a hard time believing that all these people are throwing their hands up in the air because they feel his presence. Are we all caught in a web of hypocrisy and lies?

I feel like such a complete and ignorant fool. If God is real, and if he is seeing me write this, I wonder what he is thinking. Must be really happy with me.

I'm sorry if this sounds ridiculous to you, but this is what I am feeling right now. This world is a messed up place, and I can't see, even if there is a larger plan, how anybody could dream up such a nightmare.

In the months that followed, that student and I became good friends as we walked through his nightmare together. *Why do I feel like this? Why can't I just get it?* How many times had I asked the same questions in my misery? His questions were not ridiculous; they were familiar. And what would I have had to offer that student in his darkness if I had not already faced my own?

Paul said in 2 Corinthians 1:4 that God "comforts us in all our troubles, so that we can comfort those in any trouble with the comfort we ourselves have received from God." I may never have the question "why?" answered to my liking, but I can see where the road has led me. I can see comfort in my trouble and a life of comforting others in theirs, and it is worth every minute of my trip through the night—and worth its unanswered question.

Madeleine L'Engle, in her touching memoir, *Two-Part Invention*, wrote, "We do not have to understand God's ways, or the suffering and brokenness and pain that sooner or later come to us all. But we do have to know in the very depths of our being that the ultimate end of the story, no matter how many aeons it takes, is going to be all right."

That is all I needed to know as I sat in that old, musty theater in Charlotte so long ago. It is all I ever need to know. And I do know now, in the very depths of my being, that the end of the story is going to be all right.

On occasion I will drive past my old apartment and recall its rough, dingy white walls and hear its aircraft-for-an-air-conditioner roaring into service. In time the steamrolled mucus-green carpet was ripped out and replaced with a more pleasing neutral color—all I had to do was ask—and now the apartment has passed to someone else. When I remember the desperate times there, I sit amazed at where I am now, at how the story is turning out.

I remember the radio station, and how the cracked, Christian Coalition mug in the studio outlasted every employee I knew there. I remember the showers after share-a-thon, and I thank God for where the road has led me since then. The journey has been long but beautiful, and worth it all the way.

At times I pull out Nichole Nordeman's *Wide Eyed* CD and listen again, to remember.

> *Even fields of flowers*
> *Dressing in their best because of You*
> *Knowing they are blessed to be in bloom*
> *But what about November*
> *When the air is cold and wet winds blow*
> *Do they understand why they can't grow?*

I remember the chill of November, the sense of having found myself on the dark side of sovereignty, rejected by God and left out in the cold, like a flower whose season had passed. Only recently have I realized why I never needed to fear. Nordeman's analogy was taken from Christ's Sermon on the Mount, and I had gleaned from the song that we were to Jesus like the flowers of the field: he would clothe us as he clothed them, with temporary beauty that is only for a season. But this is precisely the opposite of what Jesus said in Matthew 6:28-30:

*See how the lilies of the field grow. They do not labor
or spin. Yet I tell you that not even Solomon in all his
splendor was dressed like one of these. If that is how God
clothes the grass of the field, which is here today and
tomorrow is thrown into the fire, will he not much more
clothe you, O you of little faith?*

"Much more!" The point of the illustration was not to
show our likeness with the flowers but to draw a distinction.
We are much more to God than flowers, and his love for us
does not change with the seasons. November may come, but
we will endure. We must.

This may be the most sacred lesson of the dark night:
we must endure. Things are not always as they appear, but
we have to hang on long enough to see that. Watching *Life
Is Beautiful*, I was ready to indict God on charges of evil. Ten
years later, the view is different. I own a copy of the movie and
find no irony in the title. Despite the heartache that eventually comes to us all, life really is beautiful, but I had to hang
on long enough to see it. How many suffering people have
lost their battle for faith because they gave up the fight too
soon? We must endure.

One day, as I was reflecting on my move to Blacksburg and
regretting how awful I had behaved toward everyone during that
time, my dad said to me, "You went through that well, Son."

"But Dad," I said, "I didn't go through it well. I just sort of
went through it."

"Well," he said with grace, "sometimes all you can do is
just go through it."

"Just go through it." And don't give up.

This was my message to the congregation at NLCF on that sunny April morning in 2006 when I was ordained one of their pastors, ten years after Urbana. Tears came off and on for the two weeks prior to the ceremony as I reflected on the journey that had led me here. It had taken a decade, but I had risen from a near-fatal unbelief to a place of shepherding the church that helped save my faith. I told the crowd at my ordination, "You have no idea five or ten years down the road how you will view the circumstances you are under right now. Hang in there! Do not give up. God is able to walk you through the darkness, and he is worth going through it."

I may get to prove those words again. There may be other dark nights ahead for me. I am young still. The world is broken. And I have demonstrated an amazing capacity for depression. And since I cannot fully say what caused my sickness, neither can I rule out a relapse. I believe God intends that I live with that uncertainty. God loves humility, and the threat of storms keeps me from pride: I remember where I was, and I know it is never a long trip back there. Clouds in the distance remind me to soak up every moment in the sun. I never take a clear mind for granted when I consider the fog that overtook me—that could overtake me again.

It is a sobering truth that many who experience depression once will face it a second time later in life. But if God, in his wisdom, decides that darkness is again the path for me, then I will walk it as best I can. For now, I am simply happy to be alive, grateful that I can smile and that I can once more sing with the saints,

> *He loves me*
> *He loves me*
> *I can really say I know*
> *And I love him*
> *I love him.*

RARELY DOES A DAY pass that I am not reminded of the urgency of reaching people afflicted with depression. Always there is some new article, some new study on the disease. And some days, like today, the reminders are more personal, more painful.

This afternoon I received an e-mail from one of my co-pastors with the subject line "Sad news." A former member of my church committed suicide yesterday. I had not seen the young man in years; he moved away after graduating from Virginia Tech. He and I began attending NLCF around the same time, and though I did not know him well, I knew we both struggled with our minds. Today I cannot stop asking, *Why did I recover, and why did he not?*

Suicide statistics from one recent news article are shocking:

According to the World Health Organization, suicide rates have increased by 60 percent in the last 45 years. Suicide is now among the leading causes of death among those aged 15 to 44 for both genders.

*"Across every single country we saw there was a
significant increase in suicidal thoughts during adolescence
and young adulthood," [Harvard University researcher
Matthew] Nock said in a telephone interview.*

*He said the odds of a person committing suicide rise
sharply between the ages of 12 and 15 and the time between
the first suicidal thoughts and an actual attempt is short.*

This is not a how-to book on overcoming depression and
doubt. I am merely telling my story, passing along the hope
of my experience. But given the e-mail I received and the recent spike in suicide rates, I feel an urgency to clearly define
at least the beginnings of a path toward peace. Though the
battle with clinical depression and spiritual doubt is often a
long, hard struggle, it is not a blind fight. There are a few
steps we can take today to aid ourselves or others.

RECOGNIZE THE SYMPTOMS

The *Diagnostic and Statistical Manual of Mental Disorders, 4th
Edition* (DSM-IV) lists several symptoms that, when several of
them are present for more than two weeks, indicate clinical,
or major, depression. Here are the symptoms, so you know
what it is you are dealing with:

1. Feeling depressed—or having others notice that you seem
   depressed—most of the day

2. Lacking interest or enjoyment in normally pleasurable activities

3. Gaining or losing more than 5 percent of your body weight

within a month, or noticing an increased or decreased appetite nearly every day

4. Sleeping too much or too little

5. Feeling, *and* having others notice, that you are restless or slowed down (in speech and/or movement) nearly every day

6. Lacking normal, necessary energy nearly every day

7. Feeling worthless and/or excessively guilty

8. Struggling to concentrate or make decisions nearly every day

9. Thinking often of death and/or suicide

TELL A FEW TRUSTED FRIENDS

One major hindrance in progressing toward healing, particularly in men, is shame. It isn't easy opening up and sharing our inmost selves. We don't want others to see us as weak. But depression and doubt are stubborn foes, and we need help overcoming them. Since they are internal enemies, the struggle with them is often invisible. Even close friends and family may not see our pain. I'm still amazed at old friends from Campbell that I run into today who, after hearing my story say, "I never knew anything was wrong. I wish you had told me then." People want to help, but we must first get over our fear of letting them in.

I suggest telling a few trusted friends. It isn't necessary

that they *understand,* but that they be *understanding.* Those we confide in need not have a background in psychology or a degree in theology to help with our depression and doubt. We are not looking for answers from them, but for hope, encouragement. Of the many people I talked to during my four years of struggle, only a few understood enough to offer advice. But most were understanding, offering compassion and grace.

As best you can, avoid telling people you suspect might be harsh or simplistic in their response. And if you do receive a negative reaction, don't be discouraged. Tell someone else you think might be quicker to listen, slower to speak. Bottom line: let people in. Transparency is scary, yes, but it is a necessary first step toward healing.

FIND A SUPPORTIVE CHURCH COMMUNITY

When we're depressed, the temptation to withdraw from community is intense. A simple conversation can feel overwhelming, unbearable. Even more bitter is watching everyone else exulting in God while we sit miserably off to the side, unmoved and full of doubt. Isn't it easier, less painful, to simply avoid church altogether?

Yes, perhaps. But by avoiding fellowship, we deny ourselves one primary means by which we might find hope and healing. M. Craig Barnes sums up well the kind of community we need:

> *This is the church's task—to prevent despair from becoming a viable option by keeping the door open to the presence of our Savior. . . . So in all that it proclaims*

and does through its mission in the world, the church is
constantly fighting hopelessness.

And fighting it by compassion, not quick, easy answers
that really aren't answers at all. As with our friends, so with
our church: they should be understanding of doubt and depression, regardless how well they understand. They should
be willing to go the distance with us, even if our healing takes
months or years. Is this your church? If not, I would suggest
finding another.

Psychiatrist Dwight L. Carlson writes, in his book *Why Do
Christians Shoot Their Wounded?*

> *I have seen many dedicated Christians stymied in their*
> *spiritual and emotional growth because they don't receive*
> *the nurture of a gracious environment. Their fellowship*
> *may be doctrinally sound, but the people are harsh,*
> *legalistic and judgmental.*
>
> *It seems as though I always have one or two patients*
> *who are sincere Christians but come from very rigid*
> *churches where they do not experience grace. I generally*
> *attempt to help them grow within their fellowship. But*
> *try as they will, it seems that the fellowship stifles their*
> *lives. Sometimes the only way they can grow in their ap-*
> *preciation of God's grace is to find a body of believers who*
> *practice grace more.*

After moving to Blacksburg, my search for such a church
lasted six months, and along the way I encountered more than
my share of harsh and graceless fellowships. But the search

was worth every desperate, disappointing Sunday. Don't give up, and don't withdraw. Be relentless in your effort to find a supportive community.

SEE A DOCTOR

Whatever else it may be, depression is a physiological condition, a disease of the mind. We should treat it as such. And depressive symptoms may result from any number of other physical ailments, which can only be accurately diagnosed and properly treated by a doctor. Make an appointment. What's the worst that could happen? I spent four years searching for a spiritual answer to what was primarily a mental problem. Perhaps medical treatment would not have solved my suffering, but might it have helped? I'll never know.

Again, Dr. Carlson offers sound wisdom:

It is extremely difficult, if not impossible, to treat the psychotic, depressed, suicidal, manic-depressive or extremely anxious patient without the assistance of medications. Patients with these kinds of difficulties often come to a doctor and insist, "Get me better without medications." A diabetic would never go into an emergency room in a crisis and request treatment but demand that insulin not be used.

Dr. Carlson also suggests patience: it takes time to find just the right medication and the right dosage. I've known friends who have, under a doctor's guidance, tried several prescriptions before landing on one that worked. The trial-and-error process was endlessly frustrating but worth it in the long run.

If you and your doctor do decide on medication, resist the temptation to assume the role of psychiatrist. Many people (and almost every male) I've observed taking antidepressants at some point regret their decision to do so. Feeling weak for needing medicine, they convince themselves they are cured or that they never really needed drugs to begin with, that they're tough enough to go it alone. Without telling their doctor, or against their doctor's clear advice, they prematurely halt treatment. The consequences in all but one case I've witnessed have been negative. Depression returns, and the despair is worse than before.

Make an appointment, see a psychiatrist, and strongly consider what he or she has to say.

FIND A CHRISTIAN COUNSELOR

Medication can help, but few doctors (or their patients) would say it is a silver bullet. Almost always, counseling is necessary as well. Finding a good counselor is not as difficult as it might seem. You simply want someone who is legally licensed, committed to Christ and affirming of psychiatry when it's needed. I recommend avoiding any counselor who denigrates faith, denies the value of medication or lacks proper credentials.

Where to look first? Some larger churches now employ counselors on their staff teams. If yours does not, perhaps your pastor has developed a relationship with a Christian counselor in town. If not, try calling several pastors in your area to see who they'd suggest seeing. If even that fails, search the good old-fashioned Yellow Pages.

MAINTAIN DISCIPLINE

As best you can, maintain healthy life habits. Sleep a normal seven or eight hours, and refuse the hours-long naps that seem so necessary when depressed; they often only reinforce the dark moods. Eat regular, healthy meals: resist the urge to gorge or to abstain from food, whichever is your temptation when melancholic.

And again, as best you can—and though they may seem dry, dead and pointless—maintain spiritual disciplines. Try to pray, even if for only a few minutes a day. Read Scripture, even if you can only focus on a verse or two at a time. If you find yourself drawn to only those passages that speak of judgment, ask a trusted friend to choose your Bible reading for you, so that you get a heavy dose of grace as well. The point is to keep the communication lines open between you and God. Stubbornly refuse to let them close.

When I was at my lowest point, one well-intentioned friend suggested I stop reading the Bible for a while, at least until I could approach Scripture without the sense that God was screaming angrily at me through it. The advice made sense, but I'm glad I didn't follow it. Though the Bible was a confusing place for years, avoiding it would have only intensified the pain of estrangement from God that I felt. Psalm 13, Psalm 38, Lamentations—these were my anguished prayers in desperation. And while the answers were slow in coming, I learned through waiting the discipline of clinging to faith when faith seems far away and out of reach.

The steps I've outlined here are not quick fixes. They

are merely the first steps on a long journey. Depression and doubt are enemies that will not surrender easily, but given time, courage and persistence on our part, they will eventually retreat. Even Job found joy after his dark night, as the apostle James reflects:

> *As you know, we consider blessed those who have perseverance and have seen what the Lord finally brought about. The Lord is full of compassion and mercy. (James 5:11)*

1. Have you ever felt abandoned or rejected by God? Describe the emotions you experienced during your time of darkness.

2. Being as honest as you can, have you ever doubted God's goodness or his love—or even his existence? If so, what were the circumstances?

3. Reflect on the following either-or statement: "Either God wants to abolish evil, but can't, meaning he's not all-powerful, or he can abolish evil but does not want to, meaning he's not good." Have you ever felt like God was either not powerful or not good?

4. Have you ever experienced a prolonged period (at least two weeks) where you felt sad most of the time and didn't seem to enjoy the things you once enjoyed? How did you handle (or are you handling) that experience?

   In light of Matt's story, what steps are you inclined to take to address your sadness?

5. What qualifies a person as a "safe" confidante for people who struggle with depression?

Who is a safe person, or who are safe people, that you think you could talk to about such experiences?

6. Do you think your darkness is more physical, psychological or spiritual?

If, as Matt's professor pointed out, depression always has a physical component, and if depression is most often helped by medication *and* counseling, what steps can you take to try to move into the light?

What steps can you take to make sure you're nourishing your spiritual life (e.g., Bible reading, prayer, seeking pastoral counsel, engaging in specific spiritual disciplines)?

7. As Matt recounted his experience of gradual healing, what encouraged you? Did anything in particular resonate with your experience or encourage you to keep going?

8. If you've struggled with issues surrounding divine providence and sovereignty, did Matt reach any conclusions that resonate with or are comforting to you? If so, what?

9. What steps can you take (e.g., talking to a pastor, Bible professor or friend further along in the journey of faith, reading a particular book or getting further schooling) to try to reconcile statements made by other people or statements in the Bible that bother you or seem to conflict?

What steps can you honestly take to try to live in the mystery of God's seeming paradoxes?

PRAY

Finally, reflect on this statement by Alister McGrath: "[Doubt is] not *unbelief*—the decision not to have faith in God. Unbelief is an act of will, rather than a difficulty in understanding. . . . Faith and doubt aren't mutually exclusive—but faith and unbelief are." If your level of faith allows it, take your doubts to God and ask him to reveal truth to you—no matter how long it takes.

QUESTIONS FOR GROUP DISCUSSION

1. Have you ever doubted that God was good but been afraid to tell anyone? How did you deal with those doubts?

2. Matt was stuck on the question of how God could be good if he chose to save some but not others? What are the questions that cause you to doubt?

3. How do our personalities affect the way we view God? How do we keep ourselves from making God in our own image?

4. Have there been dark times in your life about which you still ask, "Why?" What helps you deal with the unanswered question?

5. Have you ever had someone offer simplistic answers to complicated problems, like the person who told Matt, "Sin is sin is sin, brother!" Have you ever done that to someone else? What causes us to respond this way when people share their struggles?

6. Who in your life encourages you, as Jim encouraged Matt, to see the fruit at the end of your struggles?

7. How can you, as the apostle Paul writes in 2 Corinthians 1:3-4, comfort the hurting people around you with the comfort you have received from God?

8. Matt describes things that helped him persevere through his final year of college. What are some simple, sustaining graces in your life?

9. How has a significant trial changed you? What has been the good fruit that has resulted from that time?

10. What are some ways we give "unhindered cooperation" to Satan during times of depression and doubt? How can we oppose him instead?

11. After reading Matt's story, what lessons do you most want to remember?

Acknowledgments

PRODUCING THIS BOOK WAS very much a group effort. My name appears on its cover, but many wonderful people shared in its creation. They deserve, and forever have, my thanks:

The entire team at InterVarsity Press—Dave Zimmerman, my editor, who took a chance on this book (and its author) and made every step toward publication a pleasure; Elaina Whittenhall, who championed this book early on and provided many helpful suggestions that strengthened the work; Renada Arens for encouragement and an insightful review; Matt Smith for a wonderful cover; and Andrew Bronson, my advocate in sales and marketing, for his enthusiasm.

Jim Pace, who saw this book on his shelf years before it was written, while I was still in the midst of the struggle it would recount. At last, his faith is sight.

Laura Hannum, who read the initial (and extremely rough) drafts of each chapter. Her thoughtful, honest comments were invaluable, as was her patience with my chronic self-doubt.

Chris Backert for getting the ball rolling toward finding a publisher.

Brian McLaren for his extreme generosity and unquenchable optimism. I'd still be knocking on editors' doors if not for his help.

Denny Boultinghouse, Tony Jones, Angela Scheff, Greg Daniel, Andrea Christian and Don Pape for advice and encouragement. They kept me moving forward.

And friends too numerous to name here. Thank you for believing.

Notes

Chapter 1: Losing God

p. 22   "He loves me": Tommy Walker, "He Loves Me" (Doulos Publishing, 1992).

Chapter 2: Rejected by God

p. 28   "I love him": Tommy Walker, "He Loves Me" (Doulos Publishing, 1992).

Chapter 3: The Dark Side of Sovereignty

p. 35   "Sooner or later I must": C. S. Lewis, *A Grief Observed* (New York: HarperCollins, 1961), p. 42.

p. 43   "hidden epidemic of despair": Julie Scelfo, "Men and Depression: Facing Darkness," *Newsweek*, February 26, 2007, p. 44.

Chapter 4: Sustaining Graces

p. 55   "The sense of depravity": Oswald Chambers, quoted in David McCasland, *Abandoned to God* (Grand Rapids: Discovery House, 1993), pp. 73, 84.

p. 55   "For four years": Ibid., p. 73.

pp. 55-57   "God will not hold us": A. W. Tozer, *The Pursuit of God* (Camp Hill, Penn.: Christian Publications, 1982), p. 64.

p. 58   "Jesus ready stands to": Joseph Hart, "Come Ye Sinners, Poor and Needy," 1759 <www.cyberhymnal.org/htm/c/o/m/comeyspn.htm>.

p. 59   "He is able": Ibid.

Chapter 5: Isolation

p. 73   "There are times when": George Matheson, quoted in Mrs. Charles E. Cowman, *Streams in the Desert* (Grand Rapids: Zondervan, 1925), p. 235.

p. 75   "Even fields of flowers": Nichole Nordeman, "To Say Thanks" (Ariose Music/Mark Hammond Music, 1998).

p. 77   "Every year, more than 30,000": National Institute of Mental Health Page, "Suicide in the U.S.: Statistics and Prevention" <www.nimh.nih.gov/publicat/harmsway.cfm>.

Chapter 6: Search for a Cause

p. 81   "Despite what had happened": Philip Yancey, *Disappointment with God* (Grand Rapids: Zondervan, 1988), pp. 251, 280.

Chapter 8: Signs of Light

p. 114   "Reality, looked at steadily": C. S. Lewis, *A Grief Observed* (New York: HarperCollins, 1961), p. 40.

p. 116   "Saints become saints": Philip Yancey, *Disappointment with God* (Grand Rapids: Zondervan, 1988), p. 244.

p. 117   "Job saw the darkest": Ibid., p. 251.

p. 117   "There was no sudden": Lewis, *A Grief Observed,* p. 73.

p. 123   "Nothing but the overruling": Oswald Chambers, quoted in David McCasland, *Abandoned to God* (Grand Rapids: Discovery House, 1993), p. 73.

Chapter 9: Embracing Mystery

p. 131   "God will not hold us": A. W. Tozer, *The Pursuit of God* (Camp Hill, Penn.: Christian Publications, 1982), p. 64.

p. 132   "Holy, You are still holy": Rita Springer, "You Are Still Holy" (Mercy Publishing, 1998).

pp. 132-33   "Sometimes I fear": Aaron Tate, "Prove Me Wrong" (Cumbee Road Music, 2000).

p. 134   "Heaven will solve our problems": C. S. Lewis, *A Grief Observed* (New York: HarperCollins, 1961), p. 83.

Chapter 10: After the Storm

p. 138   "a combination of nature": Dwight L. Carlson, M.D., *Why Do Christians Shoot Their Wounded?* (Downers Grove, Ill.: InterVarsity Press, 1994), p. 54.

p. 143   "we do not have to understand": Madeleine L'Engle, *Two-Part Invention: The Story of a Marriage* (New York: Harper-Collins, 1988), p. 152.

p. 144   "Even fields of flowers": Nichole Nordeman, "To Say Thanks" (Ariose Music/Mark Hammond Music, 1998).

p. 147   "He loves me": Tommy Walker, "He Loves Me" (Doulos Publishing, 1992).

Appendix: Steps Toward Healing

pp. 149-50   "According to the World": MSNBC, "Suicide Risks Shared Across Borders " <www.msnbc.msn.com/id/22949934/>.

p. 152   "This is the church's task": M. Craig Barnes, *Sacred Thirst* (Grand Rapids: Zondervan, 2001), p. 133.

p. 153   "I have seen many": Dwight L. Carlson, M.D., *Why Do Christians Shoot Their Wounded?* (Downers Grove, Ill.: InterVarsity Press, 1994), pp. 139-40.

p. 154   "It is extremely difficult": Ibid., pp. 147-48.

Questions for Personal Reflection

p. 161   "[Doubt is] not *unbelief*": Alister McGrath, *Doubting* (Downers Grove, Ill.: InterVarsity Press, 2006), pp. 13-14.

LIKEWISE. *Go and do.*

A man comes across an ancient enemy, beaten and
left for dead. He lifts the wounded man onto the
back of a donkey and takes him to an inn to tend to
the man's recovery. Jesus tells this story and instructs
those who are listening to "go and do likewise."

Likewise books explore a compassionate, active faith
lived out in real time. When we're skeptical about the
status quo, Likewise books challenge us to create culture responsibly. When we're confused about who we
are and what we're supposed to be doing, Likewise
books help us listen for God's voice. When we're
discouraged by the troubled world we've inherited,
Likewise books encourage us to hold onto hope.

In this life we will face challenges that demand our
response. Likewise books face those challenges with
us so we can act on faith.

likewisebooks.com